BRITISH TROLLEYBUS SYSTEMS
LANCASHIRE, NORTHERN IRELAND, SCOTLAND AND NORTHERN ENGLAND

An Historic Overview

BRITISH TROLLEYBUS SYSTEMS
LANCASHIRE, NORTHERN IRELAND, SCOTLAND AND NORTHERN ENGLAND

An Historic Overview

PETER WALLER

British Trolleybus Systems – Lancashire, Northern Ireland, Scotland and Northern England

First published in Great Britain in 2022 by
Pen and Sword Transport
An imprint of
Pen & Sword Books Ltd.
Yorkshire - Philadelphia

Copyright © Peter Waller, 2022

ISBN 978 1 39902 252 1

The right of Peter Waller to be identified as Author of this work has been asserted by him in accordance with the Copyright, Designs and Patents Act 1988.

A CIP catalogue record for this book is available from the British Library.

All rights reserved. No part of this book may be reproduced or transmitted in any form or by any means, electronic or mechanical including photocopying, recording or by any information storage and retrieval system, without permission from the Publisher in writing.

Typeset in 11/13 Palatino by SJmagic DESIGN SERVICES, India.

Printed and bound by Printworks Global Ltd, London/Hong Kong.

Pen & Sword Books Ltd incorporates the Imprints of Pen & Sword Books Archaeology, Atlas, Aviation, Battleground, Discovery, Family History, History, Maritime, Military, Naval, Politics, Railways, Select, Transport, True Crime, Fiction, Frontline Books, Leo Cooper, Praetorian Press, Seaforth Publishing, Wharncliffe and White Owl.

For a complete list of Pen & Sword titles please contact

PEN & SWORD BOOKS LIMITED
47 Church Street, Barnsley, South Yorkshire, S70 2AS, England
E-mail: enquiries@pen-and-sword.co.uk
Website: www.pen-and-sword.co.uk

or

PEN AND SWORD BOOKS
1950 Lawrence Rd, Havertown, PA 19083, USA
E-mail: Uspen-and-sword@casematepublishers.com
Website: www.penandswordbooks.com

CONTENTS

Abbreviations 6

Acknowledgements 7

Author's Note 7

Introduction 8

Ashton-Under-Lyne 12

Belfast 21

Darlington 33

Dundee 45

Glasgow 48

Manchester 59

Newcastle Upon Tyne 72

Oldham 89

Ramsbottom 91

St Helens 95

South Lancashire Transport 104

South Shields 114

Stockport 125

West Hartlepool 127

Wigan 132

Bibliography 134

ABBREVIATIONS

ADC	Associated Daimler Co
AEC	Associated Equipment Co
BAMC	Blackburn Aeroplane & Motor Co Ltd
BCT	Bradford City Tramways
BET	British Electric Traction
BRCW	Birmingham Railway Carriage & Wagon Co Ltd
BTA	Bradford Trolleybus Association
BTH	British Thomson-Houston
BTS	British Trolleybus Society
BUT	British United Traction
Dodson	Christopher Dodson Ltd
EE	English Electric
EMB	Electro-Mechanical Brake Co Ltd
GEC	General Electric Co
GRCW	Gloucester Railway Carriage & Wagon Co Ltd
HN	Hurst Nelson
LCC	London County Council
LCT	Leeds City Tramways
LGOC	London General Omnibus Co
LMS	London, Midland & Scottish Railway
LRTL	Light Railway Transport League
LTHS	Leeds Transport Historical Society
LUT	London United Tramways
MCCW	Metropolitan-Cammell Carriage & Wagon Co Ltd
MET	Metropolitan Electric Tramways
MTMS	Manchester Transport Museum Society
NCB	Northern Coachbuilders Ltd
NTA	National Trolleybus Association
PR	Park Royal
PTE	Passenger Transport Executive
RET	RET Construction Co Ltd
RLFC	Rugby League Football Club
Roe	Charles H. Roe Ltd
RS&J	Ransomes, Sims & Jefferies
RTS	Reading Transport Society (later British Trolleybus Society)
South Met	South Metropolitan Electric Tramways & Lighting Co
TRTB	Teesside Railless Traction Board
UCC	United Construction & Finance Co
UDC	Urban District Council

ACKNOWLEDGEMENTS

This is one of four volumes that, between them, cover all of the trolleybus operators of the British Isles. The majority of the images used are drawn from the collection of the Online Transport Archive, which is a registered charity devoted to the preservation and conservation of images of primarily transport interest. Further information about the archive can be found at its website: www.onlinetransportarchive.org. I am grateful to the following for additional images and, in certain cases, for reading through and making comment on part or all of the manuscript: Colin Barker, Paul Fox, Tony Fox, Dave Hall, Philip Kirk, Geoff Lumb, Mike Maybin and Hugh Taylor. It goes without saying that any errors are those of the author and please let him know via the publishers so that these can be corrected in any second or subsequent editions of the books.

AUTHOR'S NOTE

Within the specifications for each volume, each system history can only be a brief resume of the story; there are an increasing number of highly-detailed fleet histories and details of many of these can be found in the bibliography. Throughout the book, I have referred to 'trolleybuses'; in the early history they were often referred to as 'tracklesses' or 'trackless trams' whilst a further alternative was 'trolley vehicles'. For the sake of consistency, I have used the word 'trolleybus' throughout except when citing contemporary documentation when the original wording has been maintained. The maps are purely indicative of each network; one of the factors that made trolleybuses a popular alternative to the tram was the relative ease of erecting overhead and so many junctions and roads, particularly in town or city centres, varied over time. The maps thus show all roads that had – at some stage – trolleybus overhead; as a result, more complex systems will show sections that were not operated simultaneously. For example, with Bradford, the routes to Bolton Woods and Frizinghall, both closed in the early 1930s, are shown alongside routes such as those to Buttershaw, Holme Wood and Wibsey that opened between 1955 and 1960. There is a similar issue with route numbers; many operators did not use route letters or number originally and over a period of time the routes that did operate could change both in terms of termini and route number. The photographs used in this book have come from a variety of sources. Wherever possible contributors have been identified, although some images may have been used without the correct attribution, and every effort made to try and identify current copyright holders in the event of the original photographer having deceased. In the event of any incorrect attribution, apologies are offered; full credit will be given in any future edition. Should this be the case, please make contact with author via the publishers.

INTRODUCTION

This is one of four volumes that will examine the history of all of the trolleybus operators in the British Isles. This one describes those operators based in northern England, Scotland and Northern Ireland.

Although the history of the trolleybus stretches back to early experiments in 1882 undertaken by Ernst Werner Siemens in Berlin it was not until the first decade of the twentieth century that interest in the British Isles was first to emerge. By this time the familiar system of parallel overhead wires with rigid trolleypoles, as pioneered by Max Schiemann in 1904, had come to dominate although there were other systems – such as the Cedes-Stoll, Lloyd-Kohler and Filovia – that also had their exponents and were to influence the development of a number of – short-lived – British systems. Before the introduction of trolleybuses to a number of British operators, delegations, particularly in the early days, travelled to Europe to see this new type of transport in operation.

Although Bradford and Leeds had the honour of opening Britain's first public trolleybus services in June 1911, there had been a number of experimental uses of the trolleybus prior to that date. An earlier generation of public transport – the tramway – had been established through a legislative framework following the Tramways Act of 1870 and much of the development of the trolleybus was also influenced by the law. The 1870 Act made the tramway operator responsible for the maintenance of the road surface stretching to a distance of eighteen inches outside the outer running rail on both sides and, for a period, there was a possibility that a similar cost burden might have been laid on trolleybus operators. This would undoubtedly have made most trolleybus installations prohibitively expensive and thus weakened the case for their introduction. Ironically, however, it was the state of these ill-maintained roads allied to the use of solid-tyred vehicles that represented the Achilles' heel for many of the early operators and led to many early casualties. Although the pneumatic tyre had been originally developed in the 1880s, it was not until the late 1920s that they were routinely fitted to trolleybuses.

When the trolleybus first appeared on Britain's streets there was no concept that it might replace the tram. The trolleybus represented a low-cost means of supplementing existing tram services on lightly trafficked routes and to provide links to communities that were not well served by existing services. There was also a belief that, in certain cases, the introduction of a trolleybus service would be a useful guide to potential traffic and thus be used as a precursor to the introduction of trams. The seating capacity of the new vehicles was severely limited – the first two vehicles in Bradford, for example, could accommodate twenty-eight seated passengers each – when a contemporary double-deck tram's capacity was double that. Moreover, fitted with conventional tramway controllers, trolleybuses were also cumbersome to drive.

It was the development of the first two fully-enclosed double-deck trolleybuses – Nos 521 and 522 – by Bradford Corporation in 1920 and 1922 that established, for the first time, the trolleybus as a serious competitor to the tram. For Britain's tramway operators, which had emerged from the First World War with a backlog of track and overhead maintenance allied to increasingly aged trams, the trolleybus seemed an ideal compromise for replacing the trams: they made use of much of the existing infrastructure – such as the output from the local power station – whilst were cheaper to operate and maintain. The pivotal point here was the decision in Birmingham to convert the Nechells tram route to trolleybus operation; when trolleybuses were introduced on 27 November 1922, this was the first service where trams had been supplanted. Over the succeeding months, a number of delegations visited Birmingham to see the Nechells route in operation and many of these subsequently adopted the trolleybus.

Although a significant number of operators looked at the possibility of introducing trolleybuses, the actual number of operators that made the trolleybus their primary means of public transport was limited. In his, ultimately futile, attempt to dissuade Cardiff Corporation from adopting the trolleybus, William Forbes the general manager came up with some telling statistics in the mid-1930s. He noted that seventy-four tramway systems had been abandoned between September 1931 and September 1937; of these, only eleven had adopted the trolleybus. Moreover, ten trolleybus systems had been converted to motorbus in the period since 1925. The adoption by the London Passenger Transport Board of the trolleybus for its tramway conversion programme was perhaps crucial in maintaining the viability of the trolleybus as a commercially attractive replacement (just as a generation later, the decision to phase the trolleybus out of service in the Metropolis probably sounded its death-knell).

The role of the individual cannot be overstated in the development of the trolleybus. Bradford was fortunate in that both Christopher John Spencer and his successor Richard Henry Wilkinson, appointed when the former moved to London (and played a pivotal role in the development of electric transport there subsequently), were both keen exponents of the trolleybus. Another similar figure was Charles Owen Silver, the general manager at Wolverhampton, who oversaw the development of the trolleybus network. Sometimes – as in the case of William Forbes at Cardiff and Stuart Pilcher at Manchester – the powers that be went over the opposition of the manager to see the introduction of trolleybuses. Later on, it was the vision, for example, of Chaceley Thornton Humpidge at Bradford and Ronald Edgley Cox at Walsall that saw some of the longer surviving systems prosper when others were being abandoned. However, for each Humpidge and Cox there were multiple figures like John C. Wake (who oversaw the conversions of both St Helens and Nottingham and was general manager at Bradford at the crucial time in 1961/62 when the future of the system was under active debate in the light of city centre redevelopment).

That the Bradford system was faced by redevelopment was an irony in terms of the trolleybus; when first introduced, the vehicles were perceived as a flexible alternative to the inflexible tram. Indeed, many early promotional photographs were designed to show this by recording vehicles undertaking dramatic overtaking movements. However, the trolleybus was still restricted, for the most part (the use of traction batteries by some operators gave some better flexibility) by its use of overhead; when one-way systems were developed or when city centres underwent wholesale redevelopment, replacement was costly. This led, in a certain number of cases, to the anachronistic – and generally short-term – operation of contraflow trolleybuses along new one-way streets. Moreover, the pressure for the construction of new housing estates in the suburbs – both to cater for slum clearance and for a growing population – meant that these were beyond the existing termini and were much more easily served by the motorbus.

One factor in the enthusiasm of many operators to adopt the trolleybus was the fact that many councils and companies also owned the power stations that generated the electricity used. There was a virtue in supporting your local power station – what today would be called vertical integration – and public transport provided a demand that made the generating of power more efficient. All this, however, was to change on 13 August 1947 when Royal Assent was given to the Electricity Act 1947. This Act saw the creation of the British Electricity Authority and, on 1 April 1948, more than 500 local authority and company owned electricity undertaking were vested into the newly Nationalised industry. There were exceptions; it was not until 1958, for example that Glasgow Corporation's Pinkston power station ceased to be municipally owned. There were two immediate consequences of the changed ownership and neither worked to the trolleybuses' advantage. Firstly, no longer could the general managers of the transport department and electricity department sit down and agree a price for the electricity used; in the future the trolleybus operators had to pay the market price. Secondly, the price of electricity rose inexorably, making the cheap diesel used by the motorbus all the more attractive.

By the 1960s, the number of suppliers of new trolleybuses had declined to only two, BUT and Sunbeam. Daimler supplied no further trolleybus chassis to British operators after the delivery of batches to Glasgow and Rotherham during 1950 and 1951. Guy Motors Ltd manufactured the last Guy-badged trolleybuses during 1949 and 1950 with a batch of 8ft 0in wide vehicles supplied – appropriately – to Wolverhampton Corporation; however, having acquired the Sunbeam Trolleybus Co Ltd in October 1948 (and closing its Moorfield Works five years later), Guy continued to produce Sunbeam-badged trolleybuses until 1966 although none were supplied to the British market after the delivery of Nos 295-303 to Bournemouth during 1962. These were the last first-generation trolleybuses supplied to any British operator. British United Traction Ltd (BUT) was a joint venture between AEC and Leyland established in 1946. Production was based, until 1948 (when due to declining demand the factory was closed), at Leyland's Kingston factory; thereafter double-deck production was based at Southall and single-deck at Leyland. Subsequently, some work was undertaken at the ex-Crossley works at Stockport. Production continued until 1964 but, by that date, the only orders were for the export market. One factor in the demise of the domestic market was the ready supply of second-hand vehicles as relatively new vehicles were disposed by some of the early post-war conversions; whilst this undoubtedly benefited operators such as Bradford and Walsall, who were able to strengthen their fleets at moderate cost, it did little to sustain the supply base.

It was not only the vehicle suppliers that disappeared; the surviving trolleybus operators needed a regular supply of replacement overhead and fittings. The decision of British Insulated Callender's Cables Ltd (BICC), one of the country's leading supplies of overhead equipment, to cease its production in the late 1960s was another factor in the final demise of the trolleybus. It became increasingly difficult to obtain spares and the condition of the overhead and trolleybuses with many fleets was poor towards their final closure. The lack of spares was often a reason cited for accelerating the final conversion, although when the author was involved in helping to recover the surviving spares from Thornbury depot following Bradford's final conversion in March 1972, there seemed to be a veritable Aladdin's Cave of fittings emerging.

Four systems survived into the 1970s; in the case of Cardiff, it more limped than survived as public services had ceased in December 1969 and only final tours operated in January 1970. Walsall had been subsumed into the West Midlands Passenger Transport Executive and whilst Edgley Cox had a senior role within the new body, it was unlikely that the trolleybus would survive long within a predominantly bus-based business. The transfer of ex-Birmingham buses saw the final elimination in two phases during 1970. The Teesside Railless Traction Board had also been integrated into a larger body – Teesside

Municipal Transport – and, despite having opened the country's last extension on 31 March 1968 and having purchased five relatively new vehicles second-hand from Reading, was to be converted in April 1971.

This left Bradford – a case of the first also being the last. In June 1971, the sixtieth anniversary of the system was celebrated. This was a much more low-key event than that which marked the fiftieth anniversary in 1961. The mood was sombre as already moves were afoot for the final conversions. Although there had been no conversions since the Wakefield Road routes were replaced by motorbuses in 1967, the Allerton route – the city's first tram-to-trolleybus conversion (in 1929) and by that date the oldest surviving trolleybus route in the country – was converted to bus operation in February 1971. Over the next twelve months, the remainder of the system disappeared until – come March 1972 – only two routes remained operational. The final weekend – Friday 24 to Sunday 26 March – saw vast numbers of enthusiasts descend on the city to pay their final respects. Was that the end of the story? It might not have been had circumstances been different. The first oil crisis of the early 1970s highlighted the vulnerability of relying on imported oil – just as the Suez Crisis had done in 1956 – and the newly created West Yorkshire Metropolitan County Council did much to try and build a case for a new system. If plans had been carried through, the first routes to have seen trolleybuses restored as part of the council's policy would have been the services to Wibsey and Buttershaw. These plans came to nought as did plans a decade or so later to reintroduce trolleybuses to Leeds as a low-cost alternative to a rapid transit scheme.

ASHTON-UNDER-LYNE

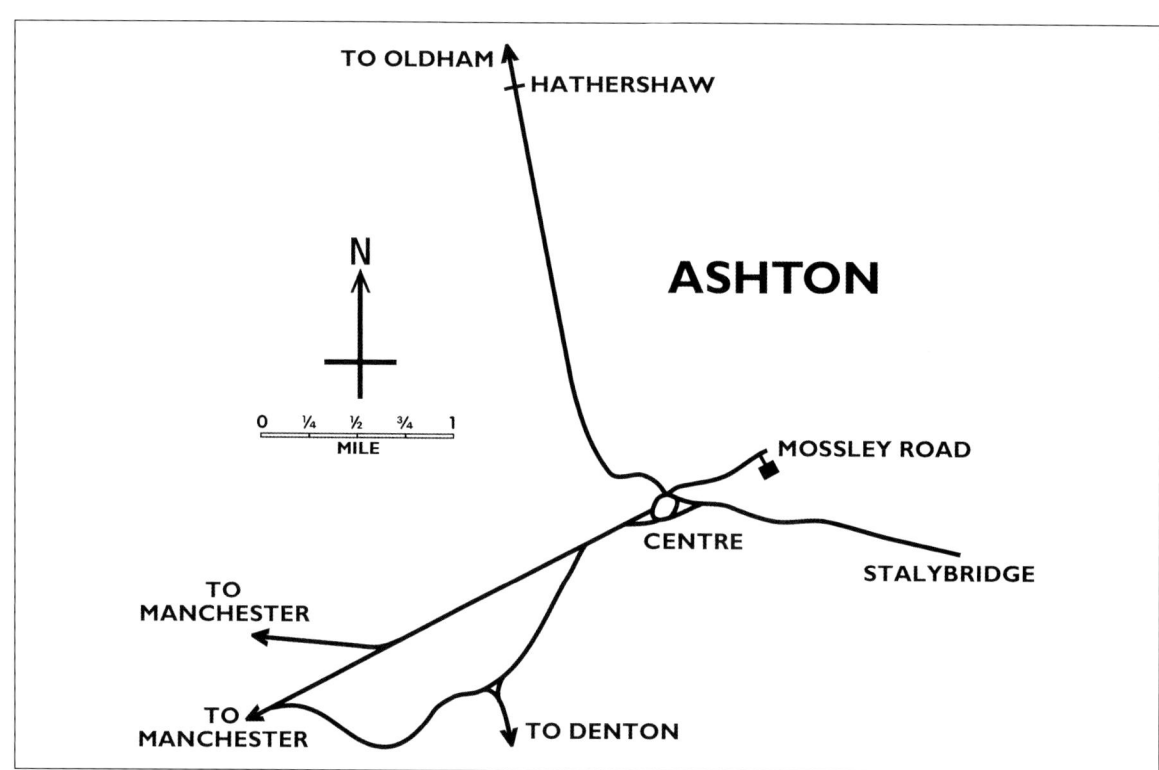

The tramway history of Ashton-under-Lyne was complex; it is sufficient to note here that the town was served for a period by two standard gauge electric tramways, that owned by the corporation and that by the Oldham, Ashton & Hyde Tramway Co (a subsidiary of BET). It was not until 2 July 1921 that the company's lines in Ashton passed to the corporation following discussions that had begun in 1914 and an agreement, following delays caused by the First World War, on 24 May 1921.

Perhaps inevitably, given the fact that the company was aware that its lease would not be renewed, the condition of the track and overhead inherited by the corporation was not great. Prior to the take-over, some repairs were carried out and a physical connection established between the ex-company lines and those of Oldham Corporation at Hathershaw; this permitted the introduction of a new through tramway service between Ashton and Oldham from the day that Ashton took over the company's assets.

However, the remedial action taken merely delayed the debate about the route's future. The track in Ashton required replacement and much of the overhead, including the traction columns, was life-expired. In addition, the growth in traffic, no doubt a consequence of the improved through service, was putting the Ashton to Hathershaw section, which was largely singe track with passing places, under additional strain.

For the introduction of services on the joint service between the town and Oldham, introduced on 26 August 1925, Ashton Corporation purchased eight Railless trolleybuses – Nos 50-57 – fitted with 36-seat bodies supplied by Short and here the penultimate of the batch is seen during 1934 in the corporation's sole depot alongside a number of the corporation's trams. The latter include Nos 28 and 32; these were two of a batch of twelve open-balcony cars – Nos 27-38 – that were built by English Electric in 1921 and were the last new double-deck trams supplied to Ashton. The initial batch of trolleybuses – of which two identical vehicles were supplied to Oldham Corporation – were all withdrawn between 1937 and 1939. *W.A. Camwell/National Tramway Museum*

Investigation of the costs of modernising the tramway as opposed to converting the route to trolleybus operation showed that the latter was about one-third cheaper, even allowing for the higher cost of trolleybus road fund licences over those for trams. On 7 August 1924, the Ashton-under-Lyne Corporation Act received the Royal Assent; this Act empowered:

> the mayor aldermen and burgesses of the borough of Ashton-under-Lyne to provide and work trolley vehicles and motor omnibuses to provide for the running of trolley vehicles between the boroughs of Ashton-under-Lyne and Oldham to extend the area of supply of the Ashton-under-Lyne Corporation for electricity purposes to confer further powers with regard to the market streets and buildings the health and good government of the borough and the consolidation of rates and for other purposes.

With the powers obtained, an order was place on 19 November 1924 for the purchase of ten single-deck trolleybuses; eight of these were allocated to Ashton with the remaining two to Oldham and work commenced in early 1925 on the erection of the overhead.

Pictured alongside Manchester No 1216 – a Crossley TDD42/1 with Crossley fifty-six-seat bodywork that was new in 1949 – Is Ashton No 49. This was the first two-axle trolleybus to be constructed by Crossley and was tested in both Oldham and Ashton – in the latter case after the body had been constructed and painted in the manufacturer's house colours of green and cream – before being purchased by Ashton in late 1937. It entered service in late 1937 and was to survive in service until 1956. *J. Joyce Collection/Online Transport Archive*

Land was acquired at Hathershaw to permit the construction of an intermediate turning circle whilst a trolley reverser was also installed at Limehurst, on Wellington Street. The first vehicle arrived on 1 June 1925 but had to be modified – aluminium replacing cast-iron spokes in the wheels due to issues of weight – and, on 12 June 1925, Colonel Alan H.L. Mount undertook the official inspection on behalf of the Board of Trade.

It was decided to launch the service when all the new vehicles had been delivered and the first public operation commenced on 26 August 1925. However, the poor quality of the road surface allied to the solid tyres of the trolleybuses led the general manager of Oldham to write on 2 July 1926 to his counterpart at Ashton, Charles Irwin Baker, giving notice that Oldham intended to terminate its trolleybus operations. Oldham, which had maintained its tram service to Hathershaw alongside the trolleybuses, was prepared to retain the trolleybus overhead within its boundaries but would substitute motorbuses for its share of the duties provided that Ashton fit pneumatic tyres to its trolleybuses. However, no agreement was reached and Oldham ceased its trolleybus operation on 5 September 1926, thereby ending the through service until buses were introduced to the route.

During 1937, three new double-deck trolleybuses were acquired from Leyland with two experimental vehicles produced by Crossley being used on test (before being eventually

In February 1940, Ashton took delivery of eight Crossley TDD4s fitted with MCCW/Crossley fifty-four-seat bodywork that were constructed to Manchester Corporation's specification. These new arrivals were designed to permit the opening of the service between Ashton and Manchester, which commenced on 27 March 1940, and that from Ashton to Denton, which followed on 1 July 1940. Here one of the batch – No 54 – stands in Piccadilly, Manchester, during August 1951 with a service to Ashton via Openshaw. Behind is Manchester No 1232. The eight Ashton vehicles were all withdrawn in 1956 or 1960; No 54 was one of two to survive until the latter year. *Phil Tatt/Online Transport Archive*

purchased). These were used both to replace and to supplement the single-deckers on the route to Hathershaw.

In 1932, Ashton decided to convert its tramway system; however, its future was closely interlinked with that of Manchester to the west. With Manchester deciding to introduce trolleybuses, agreement was reached in 1937 between the two corporations to convert the joint routes to trolleybus operation.

With work completed on the erection of the trolleybus overhead, services commenced on the Stalybridge to Manchester via Ashton and Ashton Old Road on 1 March 1938 with trolleybuses progressively replacing the trams during the course of the day; Ashton's last tram operated in the early afternoon and the honour of being the last first generation tramcar in Ashton went to a Manchester car that departed just before 4pm. Services from Ashton to Manchester via Droylsden on route 26 were temporarily replaced by motorbus until trolleybus services were introduced over the Ashton New Road section on 31 July 1938.

However, whilst investment had gone into the new routes, the original section to Hathershaw was starting to show its age and Oldham was not wiling to reintroduce the through service. As a result, it was decided to convert the 2½-mile route to motorbus operation; this was undertaken on 19 February 1939 and witnessed the final withdrawal of the last of the original single-deckers.

Towards the end of the Second World War, Ashton was allocated a batch of four Karrier Ws fitted with Utility bodywork supplied by Park Royal. Of the quartet, two – Nos 63 and 64 – were rebodied by Bond in 1955 and 1954 respectively whilst the remaining two – Nos 61 and 62 – were rebodied by Roe in 1957. Whilst the two Bond-bodied vehicles were withdrawn in 1963, the Roe-bodied pair survived until 1965. Here No 62 is pictured outside the corporation's sole depot on Mossley Road in June 1964. *Harry Luff/Online Transport Archive*

In 1946, Ashton acquired a further two Karrier Ws – this time fitted with semi-Utility bodywork supplied by Roe – and on 18 September 1953 one of the duo – No 65 – is pictured at Ashton Market. Following withdrawal in 1960, the two were sold to Bradford Corporation and were allocated the fleet numbers 820 and 821. However, due to a change of policy, neither featured in Bradford's rebodying programme and thus were sold for scrap in November 1962. *C. Carter/Online Transport Archive*

Following discussion with Manchester, it was agreed to extend the trolleybus system to serve Denton, Guide Bridge and Haughton Green. Work on these extensions was completed early in the Second World War with the service to Manchester via Guide Bridge commencing on 22 March 1940, that to Denton on 1 July 1940 with the section from Denton to Haughton Green following on 4 November 1940. With the exception of the rearrangement of the terminus as Stalybridge in 1959, the Haughton Green extension marked the final extension to the network over which the Ashton trolleybuses operated.

For the new routes of 1940, Ashton acquired eight Crossley double-deckers. In order to cater for traffic growth during the war four Utility-bodied Sunbeam Ws were delivered in 1944 and a further two Sunbeam Ws followed in 1946. Five new Crossleys were delivered in 1950.

As with the final conversion of the tramway network, the ultimate fate of Ashton's trolleybus system was closely interwoven with that of Manchester; trolleybuses represented, after the final elimination of the city's trams in 1949, a small part of a predominantly motorbus system and had never been particularly popular. The early 1950s had seen contradictory messages from Manchester – discussions about conversion countered by the purchase of new vehicles, for example – but, in September 19854, the decision to convert the Moston route in order to avoid the necessity of replacing some of the pre-war vehicles started the inevitable process of abandonment.

In 1950, Ashton took delivery of a batch of a batch of five Crossley TDD42s fitted with the same builder's fifty-six-seat bodywork. Four of the batch were withdrawn in 1963; the survivor – No 80 (which was subsequently preserved – was taken out of the service the following year. Pictured in July 1964 outside the depot is the one survivor. Ashton's depot dated back to opening in August 1902 and originally accommodated the corporation's tram fleet; now converted into a variety of commercial uses, the brick and terracotta building is still extant. *Harry Luff/Online Transport Archive*

Manchester indicated that the final routes to be converted would be the joint services between Ashton and Manchester; as a result, Ashton decided to purchase one final batch of eight new trolleybuses in order to replace the increasingly aged pre-war and early wartime vehicles whilst also completing the rebodying of the four wartime Sunbeams.

The first conversion saw the replacement of trolleybuses on the service to Haughton Green via Denton on 3 July 1960. This was followed, on 10 October 1964, by the conversion of the service to Manchester via Guide Bridge. This resulted in the operational fleet being reduced to 11: Nos 61, 62, 80 and 82-89. The final conversion occurred on 30 December 1966 when services on the two main through services – the 216 and 218 via Ashton New Road and Ashton Old Road – were converted; the last trolleybus to depart from Manchester was an Ashton vehicle – No 87 – a fitting reversal of the final tram between Ashton and Manchester 28 years earlier.

Of the Ashton fleet, Nos 80 and 87 both survive in preservation, the former part of the Greater Manchester Transport Museum collection at Boyle Street and the later based at Carlton Colville.

Recorded at the Stalybridge terminus of route is Ashton No 88 in July 1964. This was the penultimate of a batch of eight vehicles – Nos 82-89 – that were new in 1956. The BUT 9612Ts fitted with Bond-built sixty-seat bodywork were the last new trolleybuses to be acquired by the corporation and survived through to the system's final conversion on 30 December 1966. One of the batch – No 87 – was preserved on withdrawal. The 218 was one of the last two Ashton routes to survive. *Harry Luff/Online Transport Archive*

Fleet number	Registration	Chassis	Body	New	Withdrawn	Notes
50-57	TD2362/2497/3147/ 3207/3208/3262/3344	Railless LFT30 (actually constructed by Short Bros of Rochester)	Short B36C (Rebuilt as B34R between 1932 and 1936)	1925	1937-1939	
48	CTD547	Leyland TTB5	EE H56R	1937	1956	
52 and 55	CTD548-549	Leyland TB5	EE H54R	1937	1956	
49	CTD787	Crossley TDD4	MCCW/ Crossley H54R	1937	1953	Initially a Crossley test vehicle used on trial; purchased 1937
46/47	CTF313/314	Crossley TDD6	MCCW/ Crossley H68R	1938	1951	
58	CNE474	Crossley TDD6	MCCW/ Crossley H54R	1936	1955	Initially a Crossley test vehicle used on trial; purchased 1938
50, 51, 53, 54, 56, 57, 59, 60	ETE811-818	Crossley TDD4	MCCW/ Crossley H54R	1940	1954-60	
61-64	FTE645-48	Sunbeam W	PR UH56R (61/62 rebodied by Roe H61R 1957; 63/64 rebodied by Bond H61R in 1954/55)	1944	1963-65	Sold to Bradford Corporation but never entered service
65/66	FTJ401/400	Sunbeam W	Roe UH56R	1946	1960	Sold to Bradford but never entered service
77-81	LTC771-775	Crossley TDD42	Crossley H56R	1950	1963/64	80 preserved
82-89	TYE821-828	BUT 9612R	Bond H60R	1956	1966	87 preserved

Route number	From	To	Date Opened	Date Closed	Notes
14	Ashton	Hathershaw	26 August 1925	19 February 1939	Through service to Oldham until 5 September 1926
26 (216 from 1950)	Ashton	Stevenson Square (Manchester via Ashton New Road)	31 July 1938	30 December 1966	Extended to Stalybridge February 1939
28 (218 from 1950)	Stalybridge	Piccadilly (Manchester via Ashton Old Road)	1 March 1938	30 December 1966	
29 (219 from 1950)	Ashton	Piccadilly (Manchester via Guide Bridge)	22 March 1940	10 October 1964	
57 (217 from 1950)	Ashton	Denton	1 July 1940	3 July 1960	
57 (217 from 1950)	Denton	Haughton Green	4 November 1940	3 July 1960	

Ashton No 51 – pictured here outside the depot on 13 August 1950 – was one of eight Crossley TDD4s with fifty-four-seat bodywork delivered during February 1940. These new arrivals permitted the introduction of the through service linking Ashton with Manchester via Guide Bridge the following month. Of the eight, six were withdrawn in 1956 with two – Nos 51 and 54 – surviving until 1960. *Peter N. Williams/Online Transport Archive*

BELFAST

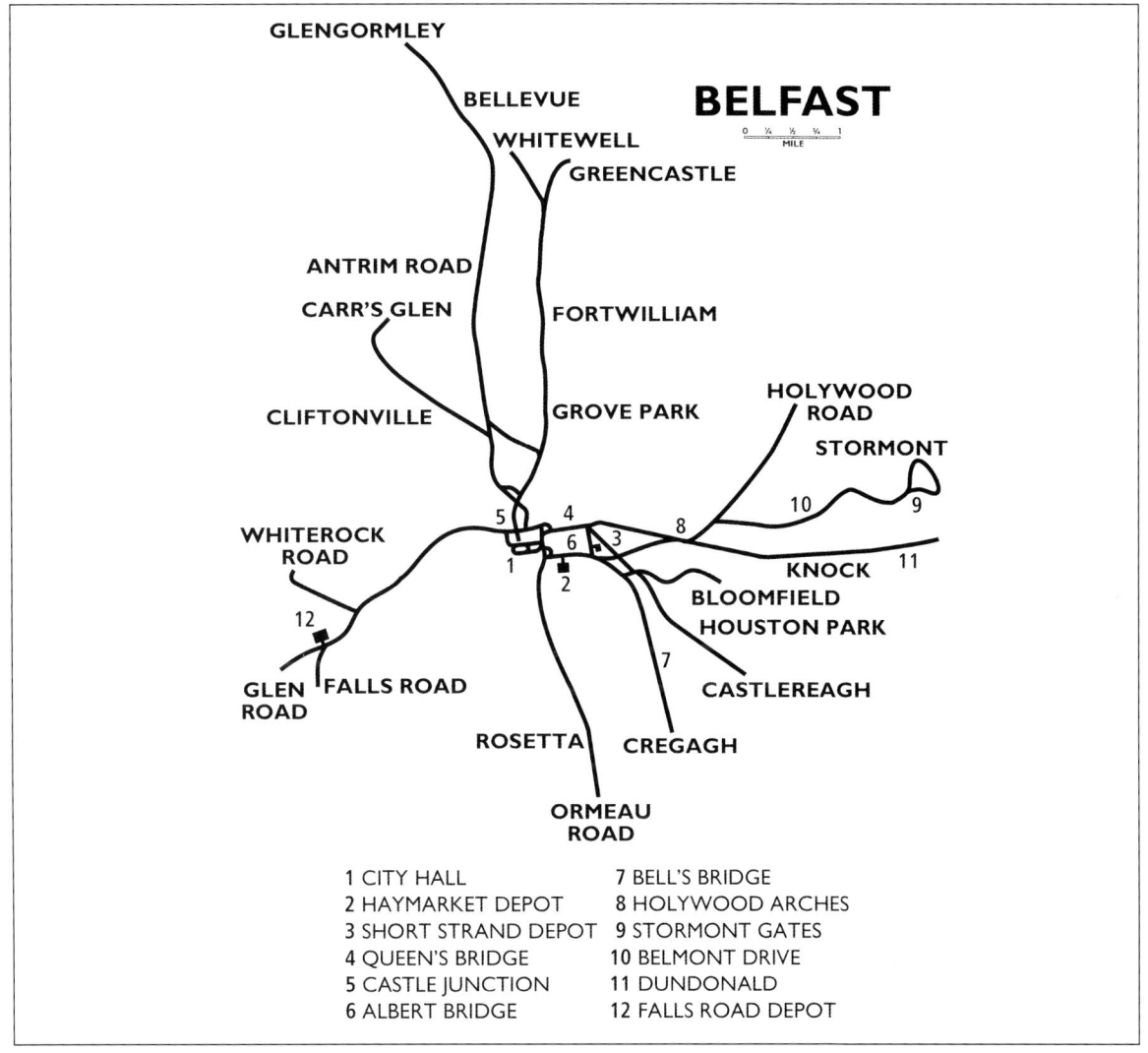

The only trolleybus system on the island of Ireland, at its peak – with some 240 vehicles – Belfast could claim to be the largest in the British Isles outside London. Belfast Corporation also had one of the largest tramway systems but, by the end of the 1920s, there were factors that suggested that the future of the trams was not rosy. The tramcar fleet was increasingly aged and suffered in comparison to the privately owned buses and, after a period of competition (the 'Bus War', which had culminated in 1928), morale within the transport department was low. Following a public inquiry into the department, the general manager Samuel Carlisle was demoted

For the opening of its trolleybus system in 1938, Belfast Corporation purchased fourteen double-deck trolleybuses; these comprised chassis supplied by no fewer than seven manufacturers with bodywork being supplied by five different contractors. The aim was to examine which combination of chassis and body was most suitable for operation. Two of these initial deliveries – Nos 7 and 8 – were Guy BTXs. The former – as illustrated here at Haymarket depot – was bodied by Park Royal whilst No 8 was bodied by Harkness. *Harry Luff/Online Transport Archive*

to Deputy General Manager to be replaced by William Chamberlain from Leeds in November 1928. The new manager instituted a major upgrade to the tram fleet, including the purchase of new trams and the refurbishment of some of the existing fleet.

In 1930, the Stormont parliament approved the Belfast Corporation Act (Northern Ireland); amongst its provisions were powers for the corporation to replace trams with trolleybuses; however, although these powers were in place it was to be a further eight years before the first trolleybuses were introduced. Chamberlain was not to be general manager for long – he returned to England in 1931 to become the first Traffic Commissioner for North West England following the creation of the role after the passing of the Road Traffic Act of 1930 – and was replaced by Major (later Colonel after his service during the Second World War) Robert McCreary, who had previously been the transport department's permanent way engineer. Although McCreary was to oversee the last new trams delivered to Belfast, he also faced the problem that much of the existing tram infrastructure was increasingly life expired.

The first section of the tram network to be converted (other than three sections [Great Georges Street, Durham Street and Ormeau Avenue] abandoned before the First World War) occurred on 1 October 1936 when the outer section of the Cregagh Road route was converted to bus operation; this was followed in 1937 by the diversion of services away from the lower Mountpottinger Road section. That year, however, was to be the tramway's peak, with a fleet of 350 vehicles covering 9.7 million miles. In 1936 McCreary produced a report in which he promoted the trolleybus as the most suitable form of transport to replace the trams – provided, he noted, that 'the Electricity Department offers and continues to offer to the transport department – its best customer – the most favourable tariff possible.' In order to test out the trolleybus, McCreary selected the Falls Road route – noting that it offered a number of advantages for a trial (including being of reasonable length, possessing an easily accessible depot for the fleet on the route, part of the existing tram track being life expired and not being interlinked with other services) – and, on 6 October 1936, approval was given to the conversion.

In order to convert the route, a contract was placed with Clough Smith & Co Ltd for the overhead whilst fourteen double-deck trolleybuses were ordered from a variety of chassis manufacturers and bodybuilders in order to gauge the most suitable for Belfast's conditions. Following the completion of the work, the new service was launched on 28 March 1938 with the then Lord Mayor, Sir Crawford McCulloch, driving the first trolleybus along Falls Road. The new service was a success, with revenue significantly higher than previously, and, following McCreary's recommendation, it was agreed on 9 January 1939 that the trams be progressively replaced by trolleybus. The first routes to be converted were those to east Belfast, to be followed by those to the south and, for the purpose, 114 new trolleybuses were ordered from AEC. The original plan had been that the entire tramway network would have been converted by 1944; however, events in Europe later in 1939 meant that the original timetable was missed.

Also recorded at Haymarket depot is No 9; this and No 10 were Harkness-bodied Karrier E6As. These were to be the only Karrier-badged trolleybuses to operate in Belfast although a number of Sunbeams were to be acquired. *Harry Luff/Online Transport Archive*

Nos T11 and T12 were Leyland TTBs fitted with the same manufacturer's sixty-eight-seat bodywork. These were to prove the only Leylands supplied to the corporation, although BUT – a joint venture between AEC and Leyland established in 1946 – was to supply a significant proportion of the trolleybuses acquired post-war. The initial batch of fourteen trolleybuses entered service with their fleet number prefixed by the letter 'T' but this was dropped with the start of the production AECs during 1940. All of original fourteen trolleybuses were withdrawn in 1958. *J. Joyce Collection/ Online Transport Archive*

The outbreak of war in September 1939 had immediate consequences; as a result of McCreary returning to military service, Samuel Carlisle returned as acting general manager. However, work on the conversion of the east Belfast routes continued although the order for new trolleybuses was reduced to eighty-eight by the Ministry of War Transport; these were delivered over a three-year period. The first route to be converted during the war was that to Cregagh via Albert Bridge on 13 February 1941 (the new depot at Haymarket designed to accommodate trolleybuses for the services to east Belfast opened on the same date); this was followed on 5 June 1941 by the route to Castlereagh via Queen's Bridge. The latter conversion saw the trolleybus services extended a distance beyond the original termini. The next service to be converted was that to Stormont – via both Albert and Queen's bridges – which opened on 26 March 1942; the service was extended from Stormont's gates to a new terminal loop at the parliament building itself at the same time. The final conversions during the war were the routes to Dundonald, with that via Queen's Bridge being introduced on 16 November 1942 and with that via Albert Bridge following on 8 March 1943. The staggered conversion was a consequence of the delayed vehicle deliveries.

With peace was restored in 1945, consideration was again given to the future; much of the tram track was in poor condition as a result of lack of maintenance and replacement during the war and McCreary, now back in post after his wartime serve, recommended conversion of the north Belfast routes in February 1946. Before work on these routes commenced, however, the remaining tram route in east Belfast was dealt with; trolleybuses replaced trams on the service to Bloomfield on 6 May 1946. The conversion had been facilitated by the delivery of twelve new trolleybuses. This was followed on 19 April 1948 by the conversion of the Ormeau Road via Cromac Street service.

Attention now turned to the north Belfast routes but both those to Glengormley and to Greencastle presented problems, particularly in terms of the terminal arrangements and McCreary was forced to seek solutions for both. In the case of the Glengormley

In January 1939, the corporation agreed to adopt a policy promoted by the general manager that the tram network be abandoned by 1944 with trolleybuses replacing them. In furtherance of this policy, a substantial order was placed with AEC for the delivery of a batch of 114 AEC 664Ts for the conversion of the east Belfast routes. However, these plans were delayed by events in Europe and, of the trolleybuses ordered, only eighty-eight – Nos 15-102 – were received during the period from 1940 to 1943. All were fitted with 68-seat bodies built by Harkness. Their arrival did permit the expansion of the trolleybus network despite the war with the routes to Cregagh, Castlereagh and Stormont plus the two services to Dundonald all being converted between 1941 and 1943. One of the batch – No 55 – is pictured here heading outbound on Castle Street with a service on route 13 to Glen Road. All of the 664Ts were withdrawn during 1962 and 1963 with No 98 being preserved. *C. Carter/Online Transport Archive*

via Antrim Road service, which was introduced on 24 January 1949, the solution was a reversing triangle rather than a loop; in the case of the Greencastle service, the new trolleybus service, introduced on 2 October 1950, was extended beyond the original tram terminus to a new loop at Whitehouse. This new loop was outside the Belfast Transport Area and was part of the operating area controlled by the Ulster Transport Authority. Belfast was not entitled to carry passengers nor charge fares for journeys outside the Belfast Transport Area and so – until an agreement was reached in February 1952 – trolleybuses ran empty to and from the terminus over the stretch of wiring beyond the boundary. Also opened on 2 October 1950 was Short Strand depot; this provided accommodation for 80 trolleybuses and 100 motorbuses.

Pictured at the Bloomfield terminus post-1951 – the year the route was renumbered from 20 – is No 124; this was one of seventy Guy BTXs with Harkness sixty-eight-seat bodywork that were ordered for the extensions to Carr's Glen and Whitehouse. Nos 103-28/43-84 were delivered during 1948 and 1949 with the last two – Nos 185 and 186 – arriving in 1950 and were the last BTXs to be constructed. The route to Bloomfield was the first post-war tram-to-trolleybus conversion – although the overhead had been erected earlier – and was the last of the routes east of the River Lagan to be converted to trolleybus operation. The Bloomfield service was converted to bus operation on 13 October 1963. The Guy BTXs were all withdrawn between 1964 and 1968; Nos 112, 168 and 183 survive in preservation. *Harry Luff/Online Transport Archive*

The final extension to be opened during McCreary's period in control was the branch off the Antrim Road route that served Cliftonville and Carr's Glen; services were introduced on 30 April 1951. The following month, McCreary announced his retirement; he was replaced by Joseph Mackle, the rolling stock engineer. McCreary had undoubtedly been a champion of the trolleybus and electric traction – ironically, in his role as a consultant, he subsequently produced the damning report that led to the demise of the Dundee tram system in October 1956 – but his successor was a life-long bus man.

Perhaps indicative of this was the fact that, after the conversion of the Greencastle route, all the remaining tram services were replaced by motorbus. There were, however, three further significant trolleybus extensions; these were the route to Holywood Road, which opened on 24 November 1952, the branch off the Greencastle route to Whitewell, which opened on 26 April 1953, and the short extension of the Falls Road route to Casement Park, which opened on 20 June 1954. This took the trolleybus network to its maximum extent.

In 1943, Belfast took delivery of two Sunbeam Ws – Nos 129-30 (the numbering gap being explained by the 'missing' AEC 664Ts for which fleet numbers and registrations had been allocated; these were eventually used on the first post-war batch of Guy BTXs delivered in 1948) – that were fitted with Utility bodywork supplied by Park Royal. Apart from one of the original prototype vehicles No 7 – these were the only trolleybuses operated in Belfast with Park Royal bodywork. Being two-axle, the seating was limited to fifty-six and the duo remained in service until 1958. Here No 130 is pictured at Haymarket depot. The depot itself was converted from a market for trolleybus operation and originally opened on 13 February 1941; extended and enlarged six years later, it remained a trolleybus depot until 12 May 1968. Used thereafter for motorbuses, it was eventually closed and the site redeveloped for housing. *Harry Luff/Online Transport Archive*

On 1 June 1958, after less than six years of operation, the Holywood Road service was converted to motorbus temporarily to permit the construction of the Sydenham bypass; in reality, the trolleybuses were never restored. This was followed on 26 October 1958 by the conversion of the Ormeau Road service. There was a positive move in that year, however, in the purchase of No 246; this Harkness-bodied BUT was one of four prototype vehicles purchased that year – the other three were motorbuses – and was potentially the forerunner of a fleet of replacement trolleybuses. In the event, it was a one-off and destined to be the last trolleybus that Belfast acquired.

There was to be one final extension – a further branch off the Falls Road route to Whiterock Road (at its junction with Springfield Road), which opened on 18 May 1959 – but 1959 also saw the decision that the entire system was to be converted to motorbus operation. The first section to be converted was the section of the Whitehouse route beyond the junction with the Whitwell branch at Whitewell Road; this ceased operation in 1962.

The following year saw the gradual elimination of services to east Belfast. The first to be converted, on 20 January, was that to Castlereagh. This was followed on 31 March by the conversion of the services to Stormont and Dundonald. Finally, on 13 October, the routes to Cregagh and Bloomfield succumbed. Also converted on 13 October was the service to Carr's Glen via Cliftonville. There was then to be gap of more than two years before the next conversion – on 5 February 1966 – when services on the Glengormley route were converted; this service had been converted to peak hours and Saturdays only from 14 June 1965.

The final phase of the conversion programme – on 12 May 1968 – saw trolleybuses eliminated from the services to Falls Road (after just over thirty years of service), to Glen Road, to Whitewell and to Whiterock Road. Two of the three depots – Falls Road (which had been extended to become the corporation's main motorbus and trolleybus overhaul works in 1947) and Haymarket – survived to the system's final closure. Five Belfast trolleybuses survive in preservation. No 246 is based at Carlton Colville; Nos 98 and 112 at the Ulster Folk & Transport Museum, Cultra; No 168 at the Keighley Bus Museum; and No 183 at the National Transport Museum of Ireland at Howth

With the conversion of the Stormont tram route to trolleybus operation on 26 March 1942, the opportunity was taken to extend the service from the gates right up to the parliament building itself and it is in front of the impressive building that No 165 is pictured here awaiting departure on a route 23 service towards City Hall. No 165 was one of seventy Guy BTXs – Nos 103-28 and 143-86 – supplied between 1948 and early 1950 that permitted the further expansion of the system (in particular the services to Whitehouse and Carr's Glen). Again, all were bodied by Harkness and were to survive in service until between 1964 and 1968; Nos 112, 168 and 183 were preserved on withdrawal. The routes to Stormont were converted to bus operation on 31 March 1963. *Harry Luff/Online Transport Archive*

A somewhat careworn No 189 heads an impressive queue of corporation vehicles as it heads towards Glen Road with a service on route 13. The vehicle was one of forty-eight BUT 9641Ts delivered in 1950 and 1954. The first batch of twenty-four – Nos 187-210 – were all new in 1950 but the remaining twenty-four – Nos 211-34 – were slightly delayed; although the chassis were delivered in 1952, priority at Harkness was given to the construction of bus bodies for vehicles destined to facilitate the final tramway conversions. As a result, all bar No 211, which was completed in 1953, entered service during 1954. All were withdrawn between 1954 and 1968. *M.J. Uden/Online Transport Archive*

The last trolleybus to be acquired was No 246; this was a Sunbeam F4A again fitted with a Harkness-built sixty-eight-seat body. New in 1958, No 246 was the only 30ft 0in long trolleybus in the fleet and was initially considered to be the precursor for a replacement fleet of up to 100 new trolleybuses. However, the decision taken in 1959 to convert the system to bus operation meant that it was to remain unique. Withdrawn in 1968, the vehicle – seen here during an enthusiasts' tour of the system – was preserved. *M.J. Uden/Online Transport Archive*

Fleet number	Registration	Chassis	Body	New	Withdrawn	Notes
1 and 2	EZ7889/7890	AEC 664T	Harkness H68R	1938	1958	
3	EZ7891	Crossley TDD6	Crossley H68R	1938	1958	
4	EZ7891	Crossley TDD6	Harkness H68R	1938	1958	
5 and 6	EZ7893-7894	Daimler CTM6	Harkness H68R	1938	1958	
7	EZ7895	Guy BTX	PR H68R	1938	1956	
8	EZ7896	Guy BTX	Harkness H68R	1938	1958	
9 and 10	EZ7897-7898	Karrier E6A	Harkness H68R	1938	1958	
11 and 12	EZ7899-7900	Leyland TTB4	Leyland H68R	1938	1958	
13 and 14	EZ7901-7902	Sunbeam MS2	Cowieson H68R	1938	1958	
15-102	FZ7800-7887	AEC 664T	Harkness H68R	1940-43	1962-63	98 preserved
103-28	FZ7888-7913	Guy BTX	Harkness H68R	1948-49	1964-68	112 preserved
129 and 130	GZ1620-1621	Sunbeam W	PR UH56R	1943	1958	
131-42	GZ2802-2813	Sunbeam W	Harkness H68R	1946	1958-60	
143-86	GZ8507-8550	Guy BTX	Harkness H68R	1948-50	1964-68	168 and 183 preserved
187-234	GZ8551-8598	BUT 9641T	Harkness H68R	1950-54	1964-68	
235-40	DDA182/986-90	Sunbeam MF2	PR H54R	1940-42	1954-56	Ex-Wolverhampton 282/86-90; acquired 1952
241-45	DDA991-995	Sunbeam MF2	Roe H54R	1942	1954-56	Ex-Wolverhampton 291-95; acquired 1952
246	2206OI	Sunbeam F4A	Harkness H68R	1958	1968	Preserved

Route number	From	To	Date Opened	Date Closed	Notes
9 (renumbered 12 in 1951)	Castle Junction	Falls Road	28 March 1938	12 May 1968	Routes 14 and 15 were peak hour short workings to Falls Park and Cemetery respectively
8 (renumbered 33 in 1951)	Castle Junction	Cregagh	13 February 1941	13 October 1963	Route 34 was peak hour short working to Bell's Bridge
22 (renumbered 31 in 1951)	Castle Junction	Castlereagh	5 June 1941	20 January 1963	Route 32 was peak hour short working to Houston Park
26/28 (renumbered 22/23 in 1951)	Castle Junction	Stormont	26 March 1942	31 March 1963	Routes 26 and 27 were peak hour short workings to Belmont Drive
11 (renumbered 16 in 1951)	City Centre	Dundonald (via Queen's Bridge)	16 November 1942	31 March 1963	Route 18 was peak hour short working to Knock Road

Route number	From	To	Date Opened	Date Closed	Notes
13 (renumbered 17 in 1951)	City Centre	Dundonald (via Albert Bridge)	8 March 1943	31 March 1963	Route 19 was peak hour short working to Knock Road; routes 20, after 1951, and 21 were short workings to Holywood Arches
	City Centre	Chichester Street/May Street	5 June 1944	12 March 1968	
20 (renumbered 30 in 1951)	City Centre	Bloomfield	6 May 1946	13 October 1963	
16 (renumbered 37 in 1951)	City Centre	Ormeau Road	19 April 1948	26 October 1958	Route 38 was peak hour short working to Rosetta
3/4	City Centre	Glengormley	24 January 1949	5 February 1966	Routes 1 and 2 were peak hour short workings to Antrim Road; routes 5 and 6 were peak hour short workings to Bellevue;
7	City Centre	Whitehouse	2 October 1950	1962	Route 8 was peak hour short working to Fortwilliam; route 9 was short working to Grove Park; 1962 closure affected only the section of overhead from the junction with the Whitewell route to the terminus at Whitehouse
35	City Centre	Carr's Glen	30 April 1951	13 October 1963	36 was short working to Cliftonville introduced on 28 May 1951
13	City Centre	Glen Road	16 April 1952	12 May 1968	
		Donegall Quay	21 September 1952	31 March 1963	One-way system in city centre
25	City Centre	Holywood Road	24 November 1952	1 June 1958	
		Cromac Square	19 April 1953	12 May 1968	One-way system in city centre
10	City Centre	Whitewell	26 April 1953	12 May 1968	Spur opened from Shore Road
12	Falls Road	Casement Park	20 June 1954	12 May 1968	
11 (renumbered 45 in 1951 and renumbered back to 11 in 1962)	City Centre	Whiterock Road	18 May 1959	12 May 1968	Spur opened from the cemetery

Pictured at the Castlereagh terminus of route 31 is No 128, one of the Guy BTXs with Harkness bodywork supplied between 1948 and 1950. The route from Castle Junction to Castlereagh was converted to trolleybus operation on 5 June 1941; originally route 22, the service was renumbered 31 in 1951. It was a relatively early casualty, being converted to motorbus operation in January 1963.
Harry Luff/Online Transport Archive

No 199, one of the BUT 9641Ts delivered between 1950 and 1954 with Harkness bodywork, is seen at Haymarket depot alongside No 51, one of the AEC 664Ts, also fitted with Harkness bodywork, that were supplied between 1940 and 1943.
Harry Luff/Online Transport Archive

DARLINGTON

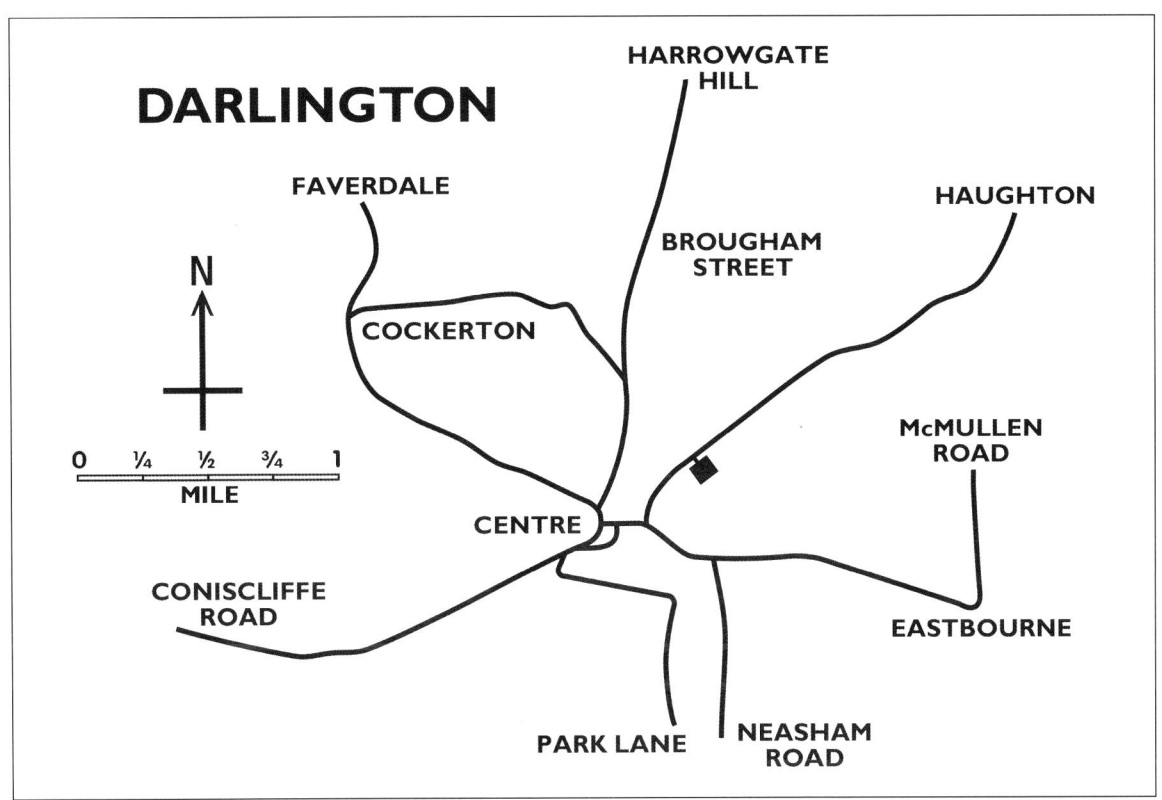

On 1 June 1904, Darlington Corporation introduced the first of its 3ft 6in-gauge electric tramways. Eventually the network extended over almost five route miles although a proposed extension from Barton Street to Haughton – authorised originally in 1902 and with powers renewed as late as 1924 – was never constructed. Like many smaller tramways, the First World War left Darlington's system in a relatively parlous condition due to lack of maintenance. In 1924, the Birmingham general manager, Alfred Baker, was brought in as a consultant. He noted that the bulk of existing track required replacement within three years but that the costs of replacement, extension and new vehicles would be of the order of £280,000 – well beyond what was economic. He recommended replacement by trolleybus; this was to earn a modest profit, cost less per mile to operate than the replacement by motorbus and maintain use of the corporation's power station.

Commercial Motor in December 1924 noted:

The Darlington Corporation is to be congratulated upon the go-a-head manner in which it is tackling its passenger transport problem and evincing a desire to meet the

During 1934 and 1935, Darlington acquired two batches of AEC 662Ts; those delivered in 1934 – Nos 33-40 – were fitted with thirty-two-seat bodies supplied by English Electric as seen on No 37 in Market Place heading towards Harrowgate Hill with a service on route 2 from Haughton. *R. F. Mack*

present and future requirements of its townspeople. It is anticipated that the trolleybus system will be in full operation by, or before, March 1926, and the results will be awaited with great interest.

On 7 August 1925, Royal Assent was given to the Darlington Corporation (Transport, etc) Act 1925. Following the passage of the Act, Clough, Smith & Co Ltd was contracted to erect the overhead and supply the new trolleybuses. The first of the fourteen ordered arrived in December 1925 and, on 17 January 1926, trolleybuses replaced trams on the route to Barton Street, which was extended to Haughton at the same time. The tram route to Cockerton was converted on 21 February 1926; all bar the final short section of the route was retained but the original terminus at Cockerton Green was abandoned with the new trolleybuses being extended to serve Faverdale. The final two tram routes – along Yarm Road (again extending a short distance beyond the original tram terminus at Cobden Street) and to Harrowgate Hill – were both converted on 10 April 1926.

With the completion of the tram-to-trolleybus conversion, a number of new extensions were added over the next few years. The powers to construct these were contained in the Darlington Corporation Trolley Vehicles (Additional Routes) Order Confirmation Act 1927, which received the Royal Assent on 29 July 1927, the Darlington Corporation Trolley Vehicles (Additional Routes) Order Confirmation Act 1929, which received the Royal Assent on 26 June 1929, and the Darlington Corporation Trolley Vehicles (Additional Routes) Order Confirmation Act 1931, which received the Royal Assent on 31 July 1931. The first of these to be completed was a link between the Faverdale and Harrowgate Hill routes – from Cockerton to the junction of Northgate with Station Road on 25 March

The second batch, this time of three vehicles, was new in 1935; Nos 41-43 had thirty-two-seat bodies built by Brush. One of the batch – No 42 – is seen in the depot yard towards the end of its life; all of the AECs were withdrawn during 1951 and 1952. *Harry Luff/Online Transport Archive*

1928; the completion of this section permitted the introduction of a new circular service. This was followed by the routes to Neasham Road on 6 April 1928, to Park Lane on 23 February 1930 and to Coniscliffe Road on 27 March 1932. Finally, on 5 November 1933, the Haughton route was extended to The Gatehouse. Further legislation – the Darlington Corporation Trolley Vehicles (Additional Routes) Order Confirmation Act 1936 – received the Royal Assent on 14 July 1936 but led to no further route extensions. Route numbers were introduced just before the outbreak of the Second World War.

A significant change occurred in 1937 with the retirement of J.R.P. Lunn; employed since 1904, he had combined the roles of manager of both the corporation's transport and electricity department – no doubt he regarded trolleybuses as ideal in both positions. On his retirement, the roles were split, with W.H. Penman being appointed transport manager. He had previously been employed at Perth and Lancaster.

During 1937 and 1938 Darlington took delivery of its first batch of single-deck Leyland TB5s; Nos 48-55 were fitted with Brush thirty-two-seat bodywork and here No 49 is seen outside the depot at Freemans Place in 1952, towards the end of its life. All of the first batch were withdrawn by the end of 1952 with the eight delivered in 1939 being withdrawn the following year. Freemans Place depot originally dated to 1904 and initially accommodated the corporation's electric trams. *C. Carter*

By 1935 the fleet – all single-deck at this stage – numbered forty-three in total; in 1937 four second-hand trolleybuses were acquired from Rotherham Corporation, but these were short-lived and were replaced later that year by the first of twenty Leyland TTBs that Darlington acquired between 1937 and 1940. All of the fleet was accommodated in the corporation's ex-tramway depot at Freemans Place. Between 1942 and 1944 a total of twenty-six new Karriers were delivered; this permitted the withdrawal of all the Straker Cloughs delivered during 1925 and 1926 – they were, when withdrawn, the oldest trolleybuses in Britain still in service. During the war there was a short extension – opened in December 1942 – beyond the original trolleybus terminus at Geneva Road to Lingfield Road (Eastbourne).

One factor in the use of an exclusively single-deck trolleybus fleet was the number of low railway bridges – a problem that a number of other systems suffered from – but, in June 1946, it was announced that plans were in place to lower the roads under them. This work would permit the operation of double-deck vehicles and, as a result, representatives from the town visited both Newcastle and Sunderland to inspect modern double-deckers. This resulted in the decision to acquire six BUTs fitted with East Lancs double-deck bodywork. However, due to the government's policy to prioritise export orders to help rebuild the British economy post-war, it was not until during May and June 1949 that the six were delivered.

Above: **The final** trolleybuses acquired by Darlington before the outbreak of the Second World War were eight additional Leyland TB5s fitted with Brush thirty-two-seat bodywork. New in 1939, Nos 56-63 were all withdrawn during 1953. Here No 59 is recorded in Market Place. *R.F. Mack*

Left: **With one** of the wartime Karrier Ws behind it, No 64 awaits departure with a service on route 1 towards Eastbourne. The service had been extended beyond the original terminus at Geneva Road to Eastbourne (Lingfield Road) in late 1942 and was subsequently extended to McMullen Road to serve the Patons & Baldwins factory. No 64 was one of a batch of four vehicles – Nos 64-67 – delivered in 1940. These were the third and last batch of Leyland TB5s and were fitted with East Lancs bodywork. All four were withdrawn in 1953. Normal services to Lingfield Road ceased on 16 June 1952 but the route remained extant until June 1956, primarily to serve the factory. *Harry Luff/ Online Transport Archive*

In 1942, Darlington took delivery of two English Electric single-deckers fitted with thirty-two-seat bodies supplied by East Lancs. Pictured in front of the Queen's Head on Tubwell Row on 14 September 1949 is one of the two – No 11 – that were sold to Bradford Corporation on withdrawal in 1954 along with a number of redundant Karrier Ws. However, it was dismantled for spares without re-entering service. *C. Carter/Online Transport Archive*

By the time the BUTs arrived (and efforts had been made to cancel the order), the fate of the trolleybus system had been determined. On 23 April 1947, it was decided that the trolleybuses be replaced by motorbuses. There were a number of factors that led to this decision – the need to serve new housing estates, the requirement to modernise some of the overhead and the level of traffic congestion – that were common to many of the trolleybus operators in the post-war years. The nationalisation of the corporation's Haughton Road power station in 1948 was also a potential factor.

Despite the policy to convert to motorbus operation – albeit deferred whilst the corporation waited to see if the post-war Labour government's policy extended to the nationalisation of municipal buses services – one final extension was opened. Following a contribution to the cost of erecting the overhead by the textile company Paton & Baldwins, the Eastbourne (Lingfield Road) route was extended along McMullen Road to serve a new factory being built for the company. The factory, which occupied a 140-acre site and cost £7.5 million, was opened in 1951 and employed some 4,000 at its peak. This final extension opened on 16 March 1949.

The trolleybus network now extended over almost 12½ route miles and, from 1926 to 1950, all corporation transport services had ben trolleybus operated. However, in 1950, the corporation took delivery of its first ten motorbuses – a combination of single- and

The first of the Utility-bodied Karrier Ws received by Darlington Corporation were eight delivered during 1943; these were, in fact, the first of the wartime chassis to be completed with chassis numbers 50001-08. One of the batch – No 48 – is seen here at the Neasham Road terminus prior to heading to Faverdale. This route was destined to be the last trolleybus service operated by Darlington Corporation, being converted to bus operation on 13 July 1957. All eight of this batch were withdrawn in 1954 and sold to Bradford; for a brief period, as a result of the Suez Crisis, No 24 operated as No T403 in single-deck form in Bradford and was subsequently rebodied as No 785. The other seven, however, were not to survive long in the West Riding, being dismantled for spares. *Phil Tatt/Online Transport Archive*

double-deckers supplied on Guy chassis – and a new manager – W. Mayes – was appointed. The motorbuses first entered service on 26 April 1950 on newly introduced services from Market Place to Newton Lane and from Firth Moor to Staindrop Road. Under the new manager the process of conversion began.

The first routes to be converted – on 30 November 1951 – were those to Harrowgate Hill and to The Gatehouse via Haughton. During February 1952, the six double-deckers, which had been largely restricted in use due to delays in the lowering of the railway bridges, were sold to Doncaster Corporation. The next conversion was the all-day service to Eastbourne (Lingfield Road), which succumbed on 16 June 1952; however, the peak hour only and duplicate service from the town centre to serve the Paton & Baldwins factory was to continue until June 1956.

Two sections were to be converted on 7 December 1953; these were the route to Park Land and the section of the circular route from the town centre via Northgate, Station Road and Willow Road to its junction with the route to Faverdale at Cockerton. The services from Coniscliffe Road, which had previously made use of the Willow Road section, now terminated at a new loop erected at Cockerton (Travellers Rest) for

With the substantial bulk of St John the Evangelist Church behind it, No 2 is seen towards the end of trolleybus operation in Darlington heading south with a service towards Neasham Road. No 2 was one of the first batch of Karrier Ws delivered during 1944. All survived to be withdrawn during 1956 and 1957; of the eight all bar No 9 were sold to Bradford Corporation but only three – Darlington Nos 4, 5 and 7 – were rebodied and re-entered service as Bradford Nos 786-88. The remainder – including No 2 – were dismantled for spares in October 1956. The impressive church, designed by John Middleton and completed between 1847 and 1849, was constructed to cater for the growing population as Darlington's industrial importance grew. *Ian Dunnet/Online Transport Archive*

With the Golden Hotel in the background – one of the few buildings from the trolleybus era still extant at this location – No 21 is pictured on Tubwell Row with a service towards Harrowgate Hill. No 21 was one of the Karrier Ws supplied during the Second World War. Fitted with Utility Brush-built single-deck bodies the new arrivals permitted the final withdrawal of the last of the trolleybuses delivered between 1926 and 1928. No 21 was originally new in 1945 and was one of the type that survived until the final conversion of the system in 1957. The route to Harrowgate Hill was amongst the earliest routes to close, being converted to bus operation on 30 November 1951. *Harry Luff/Online Transport Archive*

the purpose. This persisted until 30 November 1954 when the Coniscliffe Road service was converted.

The conversion of the Coniscliffe Road service left one single trolleybus route operation – that to Faverdale – with eight trolleybuses remaining in service. According to the original plans, this route was due to be converted in late 1956. However, the Suez Crisis and the consequent problems with fuel supplied led to a temporary reprieve and it was not until 31 July 1957 that the last trolleybus services operated. Of the fleet apart from the six BUTs sold to Doncaster (that eventually reached Bradford) a number of the Karrier single-deckers were sold to Bradford where nine were to be rebodied as double-deckers.

Although no Darlington trolleybus survives in preservation, three chassis – two of the BUTs and one of the Karrier Ws – that were new to Darlington do, albeit now in rebodied form as Bradford Nos 834, 835 and 792 respectively.

The last new trolleybuses acquired by Darlington Corporation were six BUT 9611Ts fitted with East Lancs bodywork that were new in 1949. These were the first double-deck trolleybuses to be acquired by the corporation and were purchased on the basis that work – not as yet undertaken when delivered – would be completed to permit double-deck vehicles to operate under low railway bridges. The six vehicles were not to operate in Darlington for long as they were sold to Doncaster (and eventually to Bradford). No 68 is recorded here with a service on route 5 towards Park Lane. Routes 4 and 5 – the Cockerton circle linked with Coniscliffe Road and Park Lane respectively – were the only routes that did not pass under any railway bridges. No 68 was to become Doncaster No 378 but was the only one of the batch not to see further service when the six were sold to Bradford. *Harry Luff/Online Transport Archive*

Fleet number	Registration	Chassis	Body	New	Withdrawn	Notes
1-24	HN4370-89/4770-4773	Straker Clough	Roe B31C	1925-26	1939-44	
25 and 26	HN6204/6203	RS&J	RS&J B32C	1928	1949	
27-32	HN6879-6884	EE	EE B32C	1929-30	1949-50	
33-40	HN9657/9658, AHN185-190	AEC 662T	EE B32C	1934	1950-51	
41-43	BHN188-190	AEC 662T	Brush B32C	1935	1951	
44	ET3217	RS&J	RS&J B32C	1922	1937	Ex-Rotherham 50 (ex-39); acquired 1937
45-47	ET4820/4818/4819	RS&J	RS&J B32C	1925	1937	Ex-Rotherham; acquired 1937
48-55	DHN231-238	Leyland TB5	Brush B32C	1937-38	1951-52	
56-63	FHN231-238	Leyland TB5	Brush B32C	1939	1953	
64-67	FHN974-977	Leyland TB5	East Lancs B32C	1940	1953	
1 and 11	GHN321/322	Karrier E4S	East Lancs B32C	1942	1953-54	11 sold to Bradford but did not enter service
17, 19, 24, 44-47, 8 (during 1953-54 44 renumbered 15, 45 renumbered 23, 46 renumbered 48 and then 1, 47 renumbered 11)	GHN401-408	Karrier W	Brush UB33C	1943	1954	Sold to Bradford; 24 operated as Bradford T403 before being rebodied as 785; 45 prepared as Bradford T404 but did not enter service; apart from T403 all scrapped without entering service
2-7, 9, 13	GHN561-568	Karrier W	Brush UB33C	1944	1956-57	2-7 and 13 sold to Bradford; 4, 5 and 7 rebodied and became Bradford 786-88; remainder scrapped
10, 12, 14, 16, 18, 20-22	GHN569-576	Karrier W	Brush UB33C	1944	1954-57	Sold to Bradford; 10, 12, 14, 20 and 21 rebodied and became Bradford 789-93; remainder scrapped; 792 preserved
68-73	LHN780-785	BUT 9611T	East Lancs H56R	1949	1952	Sold to Doncaster 378-83; sold to Bradford 69-73 rebodied as Bradford 831-35; 834 and 835 preserved

Route number	From	To	Date Opened	Date Closed	Notes
1/2	Harrowgate Hill	Town centre	10 April 1926	30 November 1951	
4/5	Cockerton	Northgate	25 March 1928	7 December 1953	Services 4 and 5 operated as a circular via Woodland Road and Willow Road; 4 ran anticlockwise whilst 5 ran clockwise
1	Yarm Road (Geneva Road	Town Centre	10 April 1926	June 1956	Normal services ceased to Lingfield Road 16 June 1952 but route used for duplicate and works traffic to McMullen Road until June 1956
1	Yarm Road (Geneva Road	Eastbourne (Lingfield Road)	December 1942	June 1956	Normal services ceased to Lingfield Road 16 June 1952 but route used for duplicate and works traffic to McMullen Road until June 1956
1	Eastbourne (Lingfield Road)	McMullen Road	16 March 1949	June 1956	Normal services ceased to Lingfield Road 16 June 1952 but route used for duplicate and works traffic to McMullen Road until June 1956
2	Haughton	Town centre	17 January 1926	30 November 1951	
2	The Gatehouse	Haughton	5 November 1933	30 November 1951	
3	Faverdale	Town Centre	21 February 1926	31 July 1957	
3	Neasham Road	Town centre	6 April 1928	31 July 1957	
4	Coniscliffe Road	Town centre	27 March 1932	30 November 1954	Following conversion of Cockerton to Northgate on 7 December 1953 route 4 terminated at Travellers Rest, Cockerton, until 30 November 1954
5	Park Lane	Town centre	23 February 1930	7 December 1953	

One the factors that affected the development of the Darlington system was the number of low railway bridges in the town. Immediately to the north of Bank Top station was the 14ft 6in headroom bridge over Parkgate. Immediately to the east of the bridge was the junction between the routes south to Neasham Road and east to Eastbourne and McMullen Road. Pictured heading towards Neasham Road and about to turn right is one of the batch of Karrier Ws fitted with Brush bodywork delivered during 1944. *Ian Dunnet/ Online Transport Archive*

Having just turned at the terminus of the Neasham Road route, located at the roundabout that forms the junction with Geneva Road and Parkside, Karrier W No 13 picks up a passenger prior to heading north with a service on route 3 towards Faverdale. No 13 was one of those sold to Bradford following withdrawal; however, it was not to re-enter service in the West Riding and was dismantled for spares. *Ian Dunnet/Online Transport Archive*

DUNDEE

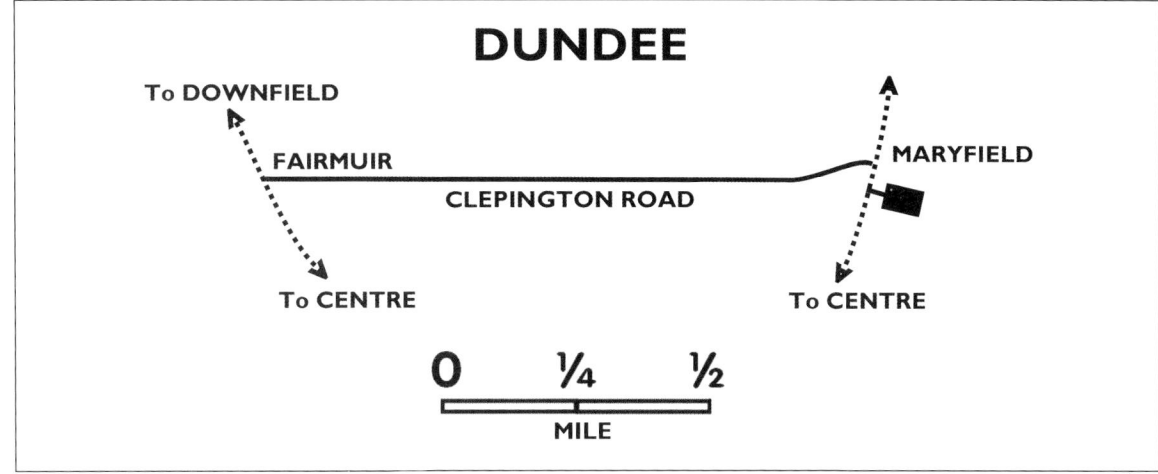

Towards the end of the first decade of the twentieth century Dundee had a thriving standard gauge tramway network; there were, however, areas that were not well covered by public tranport but which would have been prohibitively expensive to provide with tramways.

One of these areas was along Clepington Road, which linked the existing Downfield and Maryfield tram routes. The corporation, courtesy of the Dundee Corporation Confirmation Order of 1907, already had powers to operate buses – either internal combustion or electric – and so, following debate in early 1908, it was decided to pursue the latter and a party from Dundee visited three existing systems in Germany – Ahrweiler, Monheim and Mulhausen – to see trolleybuses in operation.

The deputation reported back positively and the decision on 6 August 1908 was taken to construct a route along Clepington Road as a first stage in what would have been – if constructed – a circular route linking various existing tram termini including Lochee and Ninewells. However, little was done at this stage other than abandon the concept of the circular route when it was decided not to persevere with the section along The Esplanade to Ninewells.

Three years later – on 8 August 1911 – and after the opening of the systems in Bradford and Leeds, the council reaffirmed its decision to open a trolleybus route along Clepington Road and issued contracts for the work. The total cost of the 1¼-mile route was £2,657 with work on its construction being completed in August 1912 to permit its official Board of Trade Inspection, by Lt-Col Peham George von Donop, on 3 September. This was safely negotiated and the first trolleybuses in Scotland commenced public operation of 5 September 1912.

For the new service, the corporation had acquired two single-deck vehicles; these were housed at the corporation's existing Maryfield depot, which was accessed from the loop at the eastern end of the route via a skate and the tram track and overhead.

Above: **The photographer** seems to be garnering more interest from both the children and the trolleybus crew in this view of one of Dundee's two trolleybuses – No 68 – than the vehicle itself. Given the state of the vehicle, it's probable that the view was taken early in the two-year life of the 1¼-mile single route along Clepington Road from Fairmuir, on the Downfield tram route, to Maryfield, just short of the tram terminus there. *Barry Cross Collection/Online Transport Archive*

Right: **No 68** is seen again, this time at the western terminus at Fairmuir. The two vehicles – both built by RET and fitted with twenty-eight-seat single-deck bodies supplied by Milnes Voss – were stored in Maryfield depot, where they had been based, after services ceased on 13 May 1914 prior to being sold to Halifax Corporation in January 1918. The solid tyres allied to the poor road surface led to complaints amongst both passengers and local residents along Clepington Road and resulted in the duo being nicknamed the 'Stouries'. *Barry Cross Collection/Online Transport Archive*

During his inspection, von Donop is alleged to have commented that whilst the trolleybus performed well he doubted if the route would be financially viable. This was the least of the trolleybuses problems; the unmade road surface did not handle the solid tyres of the trolleybuses well and, during particularly dry weather, clouds of dust were evident, resulting in the trolleybuses acquiring the nickname of 'The Stouries'.

By early 1914, the financial and operational problems of the route resulted in the Transport Committee deciding, on 20 April, that the service be abandoned. The trolleybuses last operated on 13 May 1914 and the two vehicles were put into store. Three years later the pair was purchased by Halifax Corporation where, after rebuilding, they re-entered service in 1921.

Fleet number	Registration	Chassis	Body	New	Withdrawn	Notes
67 and 68	N/A	Railless (manufactured by David Brown)	Milnes Voss B28R	1912	1914	Sold to Halifax 1918

Route number	From	To	Date Opened	Date Closed	Notes
N/A	Fairmuir	Maryfield	5 September 1912	13 May 1914	

A side view of one of Dundee's two trolleybuses pictured at the Maryfield terminus; the Dundee livery at the time was Indian Red with cream. Following their withdrawal and sale, the fleet numbers of the two trolleybuses were reallocated to two new double-deck trams in 1920. *Barry Cross Collection/Online Transport Archive*

GLASGOW

Scotland's second trolleybus system and the only one to open in the British Isles after the Second World War, Glasgow's network expanded to become one of the largest in the country by the late 1950s but was always overshadowed by the much larger tramway system until the latter ceased operation in September 1962.

Although thoughts about the possibility of introducing trolleybus services to act as feeders to the tram network existed in the early 1920s and powers to operate trolleybuses as tramcar replacements – on outlying routes where the costs of refurbishment were deemed prohibitive – were obtained in 1933, these were not progressed. However, the relatively few tramway conversions pre-war – such at Abbotsinch and Kilbarchan – were to bus rather than trolleybus.

At the end of the Second World War, Glasgow possessed the largest tramway system in the country; however, despite the introduction of the 'Coronation' cars in 1938, the bulk of the Glasgow tramcar fleet comprised the numerous 'Standard' type of which the oldest were almost fifty years old. Although the corporation was keen to acquire further trams – as indeed it did – the option of introducing an experimental trolleybus service was also

GLASGOW • 49

When Glasgow ordered its initial batch of trolleybuses, BUT and Metro-Cammell were producing the 'Q1' class of trolleybus for London Transport and Glasgow's Nos TB1-TB34 were identical – even down to the roundel on the front as evinced by No TB9 in original livery seen crossing Albert Bridge in 1951 – to the vehicles supplied to the metropolis. Pressure from London Transport, keen to preserve their use of the roundel, saw the roundels eventually removed. *C. Carter/Online Transport Archive*

Pictured at Hampden depot on 1 April 1962 is No TB12; this was one of the initial batch of trolleybuses supplied by BUT – the 'TB' stood for trolleybus/BUT – with which the system opened in 1949. Regulations at the time meant that the maximum length permitted for two-axle vehicles was 27ft 6in and, as these were 30ft 0in in length, they were three-axle models. Note the livery variation between No TB12, which has been spray-painted in motorbus colours (the last of four different liveries), and the vehicles alongside, including No TB17, which carry the traditional hand-painted livery. This initial batch of vehicles was withdrawn between 1960 and 1966 when the last were taken out of service following the conversion of the High Street routes. Hampden depot opened in December 1950; it was designed in such a way as to permit gravity parking and thus was not equipped with complicated overhead. *Ian Dunnet/Online Transport Archive*

considered. Plans for the conversion of service 2 – from Polmadie to Provanmill – from tram to trolleybus were formulated and, on 10 January 1946, the plans were given the go ahead by the corporation.

The operation of Glasgow trams with Fischer bow collectors rather than the more conventional trolleypole added to the complexity of the conversion particularly where the vehicles might have operated alongside each other in narrow streets. As a result, the original scheme was enlarged to include the conversion of part of tram service 10 whilst the existing tram route was extended to service new estates at Blackhill and Kings Park.

The original proposal had envisaged the purchase of twenty trolleybuses to a specified design; the decision to expand the plans resulted in a further forty-four vehicles being ordered in 1947. This meant that the initial fleet would comprise thirty-four BUT 9641Ts and thirty Daimler CTM6s; all were three-axle fitted with Metro-Cammell seventy-seat bodywork. At the time, 30ft 0in long vehicles were only permitted when fitted with three axles. All the initial sixty-four trolleybuses were delivered between February and June 1949 in the case of the BUTs and between December 1949 and August 1951 in the case of the Daimlers.

Throughout the period of formulating the proposals for the introduction of trolleybuses the general manager, E.R.L. Fitzpayne, stressed that the plans did not envisage the wholesale conversion of the tramway network; the decision to convert the entire tram system to either motorbus or trolleybus operation only came later – and by that stage the motorbus was the much-favoured alternative.

When new in 1951, Glasgow's first single-deck trolleybus – a BUT RETB1 fitted with a Weymann body – was initially numbered TB35 and it is with this number that the vehicle was recorded on Saltmarket on 22 June 1951 in its original livery. The development of the 30ft long standee trolleybus, with its twenty-six seated and forty standing capacity, owned much to the general manager's visit to a conference in Stockholm in 1949. As built, the vehicle had a rear entrance, at which the conductor sat at a pay desk to collect the fares, with a forward exit door. *C. Carter/Online Transport Archive*

Above: **Also recorded** on Saltmarket on 2 June 1951 was TD29 in its original livery. This was the penultimate of a batch of thirty vehicles – Nos TD1-30 – that were supplied by Daimler during 1949 and 1950. Fitted with MCCW bodies all were withdrawn between 1958 and 1964. *C. Carter/Online Transport Archive*

Left: **In 1953** the corporation took delivery of two batches of Sunbeams F4As; these were designated 'TG' (Trolleybus Guy – Guy Motors Ltd owned the Sunbeam trademark) and Nos TG1-5 were unique in that they were bodied by the Walter Alexander & Co (Coachbuilders) Ltd – the only trolleybus bodies that this company was to manufacture. All five were withdrawn at the end of February 1965. *Harry Luff/Online Transport Archive*

In order to facilitate the work to convert the routes to trolleybus operation, three routes were temporarily converted to bus operation in early 1949: these were the section of service 10 from Crown Street to Rutherglen on 23 January 1949 and services 2 from Polmadie to Provanmill and 19 from Springburn to either Mount Florida or Netherlee which both succumbed on 20 February 1949.

Trolleybus services commenced on service 102 from Polmadie to Riddrie on 3 April 1949 and were extended southwards from Polmadie to Hampden on 3 July 1949. Operation of service 101 – from Cathedral Street to Shawfield (on the Rutherglen route; it would not be until 19 February 1956 that services would be extended to Rutherglen, following the conversion of tram service 18 to bus operation the previous year) – commenced on 6 November 1949; this service was extended from Cathedral Street to Royston Road in August the following year.

Under Fitzpayne, Glasgow had a reputation for pioneering various potential improvements in vehicle design both for trams and for trolleybuses. The next trolleybus to be acquired was revolutionary; this was No TB35 (later No TBS1) which was a 30ft 0in-long single-decker that was designed for PAYE operation. With seats for twenty-six passengers and standing accommodation for forty (later reduced to thirty, the vehicle had the capacity equivalent to that of a contemporary 27ft 6in double-decker. The standee principle had been witnessed by Fitzpayne in Sweden during 1949 and the new vehicle was delivered in March 1951 having been displayed the previous year's Commercial Motor Show.

The second batch of Sunbeam F4As delivered in 1953 – Nos TG6-20 – were fitted with Weymann bodies. Here No TG7 is pictured on Glassford Street heading towards Clarkston with a service on route 105; the Clarkston to Queen's Cross service was destined to be the last trolleybus route in Scotland, being converted on 27 May 1967. By that date, the Sunbeams were already history; the fifteen Weymann-bodied examples were withdrawn between February 1965 and April 1966. *Richard Lomas/Online Transport Archive*

Left: **No TB35** was renumbered TBS1 (Trolleybus BUT Single-deck No 1) in 1953 and was to survive in service until 1964. Here the renumbered trolleybus is seen at the Muirend terminus of route 104 on a wet day. This view shows to good effect the two doors with which No TBS1 was originally equipped. Route 104 was destined to be the first of the Glasgow trolleybus routes to be converted to bus operation (on 6 January 1962). *Harry Luff/Online Transport Archive*

Below: **Following the** experimental use of TB35, a further ten standee single-deckers – Nos TBS2-11 – were delivered in 1953. The batch was allocated to route 104 which had been originally introduced on 31 August 1952. The new vehicles were slightly modified from No TBS1 in that the exit door was centrally located and wider than that on the prototype as evinced by this view of the nearside of No TBS2. All ten, which had been modified between 1959 and 1961, were finally withdrawn in November 1964. *Harry Luff/Online Transport Archive*

Further trolleybus services were introduced during 1952 and 1953 with both motorbus and tram routes being converted. An additional ten single-deckers were acquired in 1953; these differed slightly from No TBS1 with all being allocated to service 104 (from Muirend to Cathedral Street that had originally opened on 31 August 1952 in place of part of motorbus route 32). In addition, twenty Sunbeam F4A double-deckers also entered service that year with service 105 – from Queen's Cross to Clarkston – commencing operation on 5 July 1953; this replaced part of tram service 13.

On 26 November 1954, the corporation decided to convert a significant part of the surviving tram network in order to eliminate some 450 of the oldest of the 'Standard' cars; originally it had been proposed that all be replaced by motorbus but, in order to ensure that Pinkston Power Station (which was still corporation-owned and on which a

Glasgow's second No TB35 was the first of first of ninety BUT 9613Ts that entered service between July 1957 and January 1959. The vehicles were ordered as part of the project to convert trams routes 7 and 12 to trolleybus operation. Changed regulations meant that it was now possible to produce 30ft 0in long two-axle vehicles and these were the only two-axle trolleybuses of this length to operate on the Glasgow system. Although the bodywork was ordered from Park Royal, actual construction of the bodies was undertaken by Crossley; No TB123 was to be the last trolleybus bodied by Crossley before its factory at Stockport closed in late 1958. On 10 August 1951, No TB35 is seen crossing Victoria bridge on driver training duties. All ninety of the type were withdrawn between 1965 and 1967 during the final run down of the system; No TB78 was preserved following withdrawal, thus becoming the only double-decker from the system to survive. *R.L. Wilson/Online Transport Archive*

For the conversion of tram route 12 into trolleybus route 108 – from Paisley Road Toll to Mount Florida – a further ten single-deck trolleybuses were ordered (originally it had been hoped that twenty would have been delivered but a further ten double-deckers were obtained instead). Nos TBS12-21 were BUT RETB1s fitted with Burlingham fifty-seat bodies. At 34ft 6in in length, the ten were longer than the then legal limit for two-axle trolleybuses – 30ft 0in – and special dispensation was granted by the Ministry of Transport for their operation on route 108. The success of these vehicles was one factor in the relaxation of regulations in 1961 when 36ft 0in vehicles became legal. Here No TBS17 is pictured at the Paisley Road Toll terminus on 24 March 1966. Of the ten, No TBS13, which had been displayed at the 1958 Commercial Motor Show, was preserved as was No TBS21; unfortunately, the latter was scrapped in 2016. *Alan Murray-Rust/Online Transport Archive*

£2 million extension was opened on 3 December 1954) was still utilised, it was decided to extend further the trolleybus network.

Additional vehicles – both double- and single-deck – were ordered with a total of 100 new trolleybuses being delivered between 1957 and 1959. During 1957 and 1958 three additional services were introduced and by 1959 a total of 194 trolleybuses were in service – the peak number that the system operated. The single-deckers – again revolutionary in being 35ft 0in in length (and this required special permission to operate) – were designed for use on service 108, from Mount Florida to Paisley Road Toll, which opened on 15 November 1958 and which was destined to be the last extension and took the mileage to almost 43½ route miles.

However, the fate of the trolleybus system had, effectively, already been sealed. On 25 September 1957, the ruling Labour group on the council decided that the remaining tram services were to be converted to bus with a maximum trolleybus fleet of 200. This, combined with the decision to sell Pinkston to the South of Scotland Electricity Board (a deal concluded in 1958), meant that the 'virtuous circle' of the corporation's public transport network providing a base load for the corporation-owned power station was lost.

Two services – the 103 on 9 May 1959 and the 104 on 6 January 1962 – were withdrawn but these involved no loss of wiring as all the sections were covered by other services. However, construction work on the new Clyde tunnel resulted in the withdrawal of services from the peak hour only extensions to Shieldhall and Linthouse in late 1964 and, in mid-1965, the general manager advocated the conversion of the entire system. This became corporation policy in early 1966 and three services – the 101, 102 and 106 – were converted that year, leaving two – the 107 and 108 – to be converted on 4 March 1967. The last service – the 105 – was converted to be operation on 27 May 1967 with No TB123 acting as the official last trolleybus, having been suitably decorated for the purpose, the following day.

During its eighteen years, the Glasgow system used a number of depots – Dennistoun, Govan and Larkfield were all ex-tram depots – but the only purpose-built trolleybus depot was that at Hampden, which opened on 17 December 1950. The depot was designed in such a way as to minimise the complexity of the overhead, with gradients designed to permit the movement of vehicles in the open-air parking through gravity.

Of the Glasgow fleet, three examples were initially preserved; these included one double-decker – No TB78 – and two of the 1958-delivered single-deckers – Nos TBS13 and TBS21. Although Nos TB78 and TBS13 survive – at Sandtoft and at the Glasgow Riverside Museum respectively – sadly No TBS21 was scrapped in 2016.

No TBS1 is recorded in its final guise (and third livery); there were problems with congestion on the standee single-deckers with the result that, in 1955, their notional standing capacity was reduced to thirty. Between 1959 and 1961 all of the standee vehicles were rebuilt at Hampden as conventional single-deckers, losing their rear doors as a consequence. The modification work resulted in the seating capacity being increased to 36. No TBS1 was withdrawn in November 1964. *Ian Dunnet/Online Transport Archive*

Appropriately the last trolleybus to enter service in the city – No TB123 on 4 December 1958 – was selected to be the official last trolleybus. It is seen here, suitably bedecked, at Hampden garage on 27 May 1967 – the day before its last duties No TB105 had operated the last public service the same day; No TB78 was also decorated for the final closure prior to being preserved. *Alan Murray-Rust/Online Transport Archive*

Fleet number	Registration	Chassis	Body	New	Withdrawn	Notes
TB1-34	FYS701-734	BUT 9641T	MCCW H70R	1949	1960-66	Bodies based on a London Transport design
TD1-30	FYS735-764	Daimler CTM6	MCCW H70R	1949-50	1958-64	Bodies based on a London Transport design
TB35 (renumbered TBS1 1953)	FYS765	BUT RETB1	Weymann B26D (later reseated to 36)	1951	1964	Displayed at 1950 Commercial Motor Show
TBS2-11	FYS766-775	BUT RETB1	East Lancs B27D (rebuilt to B36C 1959-61)	1953	1964	One chassis displayed at 1952 Commercial Motor Show; one used as demonstrator at Nottingham and Walsall
TG1-5	FYS776-780	Sunbeam F4A	Alexander H62R	1953	1965	TG1 displayed at 1952 Commercial Motor Show
TG6-20	FYS781-795	Sunbeam F4A	Weymann H62R	1953	1965-66	
TB35-64	FYS796-825	BUT 9613T	Crossley H70R (reseated to H71R 1960-61)	1957	1965-67	One chassis displayed at 1956 Commercial Motor Show; TB107 displayed at 1958 Commercial Motor Show

Fleet number	Registration	Chassis	Body	New	Withdrawn	Notes
TB65-124	FYS826-875/977-986	BUT 9613T	Crossley H71R	1957-59	1966-67	TB78 preserved
TBS12-21	FYS987-996	BUT RETB1	Burlingham B50F	1958	1961-67	TBS213 (shown at 1958 Commercial Motor Show) preserved; TBS21 originally preserved but scrapped in 2016

Route number	From	To	Date Opened	Date Closed	Notes
101	Cathedral Street	Shawfield	6 November 1949	30 April 1966	
101	Shawfield	Rutherglen	19 February 1956	30 April 1966	
101	Cathedral Street	Royston Road	6 August 1950	30 April 1966	
101	Royston Road	Riddrie	2 September 1962	30 April 1966	
102	Polmadie	Riddrie	3 April 1949	30 April 1966	Cut back from Riddrie to Royston Road 2 September 1962
102 (renumbered 103 6 August 1950)	Riddrie (via Polmadie)	Hampden Park	3 July 1949	9 May 1959	
104	Cathedral Street	Muirend	31 August 1952	6 January 1962	
105	Clarkston	Queens Cross	5 July 1953	27 May 1967	Last trolleybus route in Scotland
106	Bellahouston	Millerston	15 June 1958	1 October 1966	
107	Maitland Street	Muirend	7 May 1958	4 March 1967	
108	Mount Florida	Paisley Road Toll	15 November 1958	4 March 1967	
106/108	Paisley Road Toll	Shieldhall and Linthouse	15 November 1958	14 November 1964	Peal hour and special services on routes 106 and 108 to Linthouse and Shieldhall; withdrawn as a result of construction work for Clyde tunnel
NS5	George Square	Clarkston	16 December 1956	26 November 1960	Night service

MANCHESTER

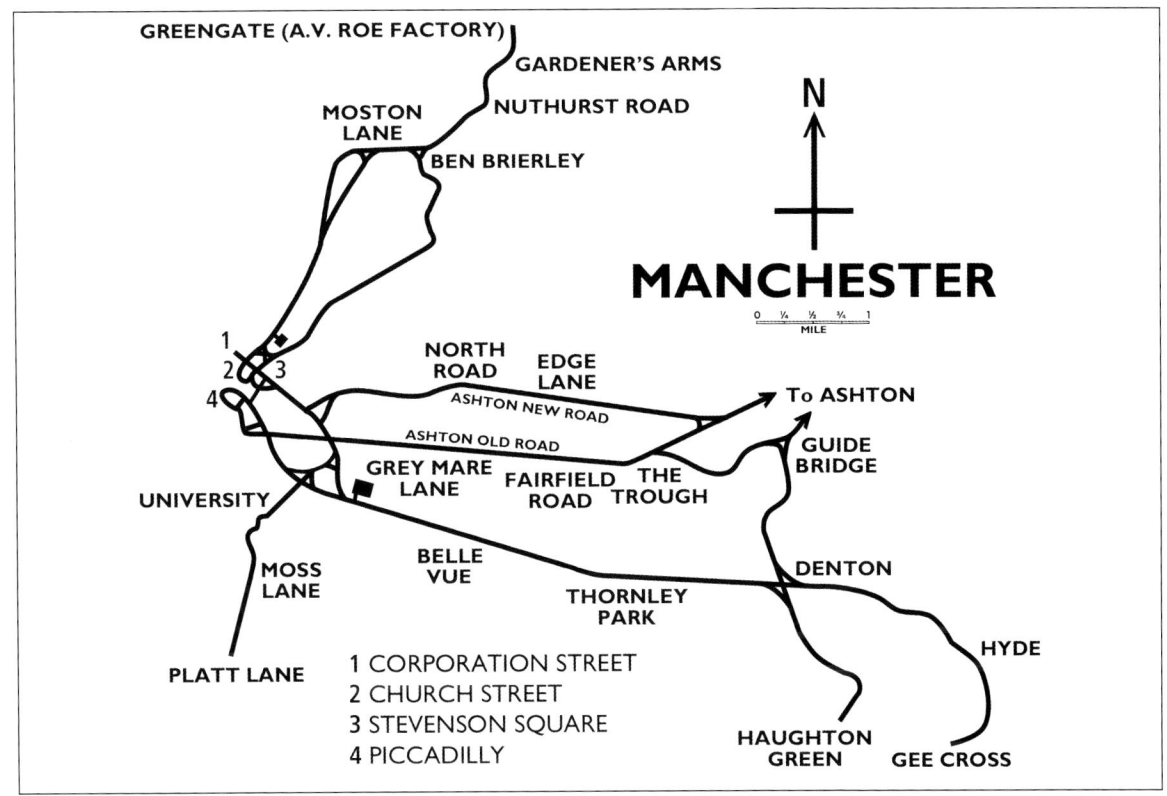

By the late 1920s Manchester possessed the third largest electric tramway in the British Isles, extending over a network of some 123 route miles operated by some 950 trams. Through services provided connections to a number of neighbouring towns and cities, including Salford, Stockport and Oldham. However, the sudden death of the general manger, Henry Mattinson, on 1 September 1928 and his eventual replacement R. Stuart Pilcher foreshadowed a change of policy.

Whilst Pilcher had been a proponent of tramway expansion and modernisation in Edinburgh, in Manchester circumstances were different. The new general manager faced an immediate challenge over the future of route 53; this service, which passed under a number of low bridges, was operated by single-deck trams and, by the late 1920s, its track was life expired. The cost of modernisation, including making it suitable for double-deck operation in order to increase capacity, was considered prohibitive and so the service was gradually converted to motorbus operation between 3 March 1930 and 6 April 1930; this conversion was followed on 26 October 1930 by the conversion of route 25 to Bradford Road. The improved financial results – increased revenue and lower operating costs – from the replacement motorbus services convinced Pilcher that the tram was dated and that the future of local public transport lay in the motorbus; as a result he became one of the most significant advocates of tram-to-motorbus conversion. Although it would not be until 7 July 1937 that the corporation finally agreed to replace all the remaining tram services – a policy that was inevitably delayed as a result of the Second World War – the period from 1931 until that date saw a significant number of tram routes converted.

There was, however, a strong group on the council which saw the trolleybus as an ideal replacement and matters came to a head in the discussions about the conversion of the tram route along Ashton Old Road. With Pilcher's strong support, the transport committee had agreed to convert the route to motorbus operation. However, a counter argument gained ground; there was a strong argument in favour of electric traction in that it used coal from British mines as opposed to imported oil whilst the trolleybus – given its relatively recent adoption in London – was perceived as a 'fashionable' means of transport.

Following a battle between the city council and the transport department, it was agreed on 31 July 1935 that powers to operate trolleybuses on the Ashton Old Road route be sought; these were granted through the Manchester Corporation Act 1936, which gained the Royal Assent on 31 July 1936 but even as late as 29 July 1936, the council was forced

For the opening of the system on 1 March 1938 (and over the succeeding months through to August 1938), Manchester Corporation acquired a total of seventy-six vehicles; thirty-eight of these were two-axle whilst the remaining thirty-eight were three-axle. All were fitted with bodywork built locally by Crossley on frames supplied by Metropolitan-Cammell Ltd. Nos 1000-027 were Crossley TDD4s that had chassis based around a modified version of an existing bus chassis produced by the company. With the Grand Hotel in the background, No 1023 is seen turning from Aytoun Street into Portland Street with a service on route 219X. The vehicle sports the post-war livery of red, with cream window surrounds and grey roof. No 1023 was withdrawn in January 1956; all the surviving members of the batch were taken out of service by the end of that month, withdrawals having commenced in March 1953. *Peter Sykes/Online Transport Archive*

to reject renewed attempts by the transport committee to use motorbuses rather than trolleybuses.

Although the initial proposal only affected the Ashton Old Road routes, the fact that they were interlinked with those that operated along Ashton New Road resulted in a decision on 3 March 1937 to convert the tram services along Ashton New Road at the same time. The first services – along Ashton Old Road – from Piccadilly to Stalybridge operated jointly with Ashton were inaugurated on 1 March 1938. In order to accommodate the trolleybuses, a new depot was opened at the same time on Rochdale Road; this could provide accommodation for 115 vehicles. The last trams operated along Ashton New Road on 30 July 1938, being replaced by trolleybuses the following day.

With the corporation's policy now being wholesale conversion of the tram network, consideration was given to which form of transport would be used in replacement. The transport department remained antagonistic towards trolleybuses, highlighting the higher operating costs, whilst also identifying a number of routes suitable for trolleybus operation. On 1 February 1939, the proposal – including further tram-to-trolleybus conversions – was approved. The next service to open was that from Piccadilly to Guide Bridge via Ashton Old Road on 16 October 1939; this was extended through to Ashton and became a further joint route on 22 March 1940.

When war broke out in September 1939, it caused some delay to the immediate programme of conversion of tram routes to trolleybus operation (with the conversion of the Gee Cross route deferred), although the problems in obtaining fuel supplies actually

Also pictured turning right from Aytoun Street into Portland Street is No 1037; this was the last of a batch of ten Leyland TB4s – Nos 1028-37 – which were all new in March 1938. Based primarily at Rochdale Road, the batch was used on services to Moston and Ashton. The first two were taken out of service during 1951 and all had been withdrawn by the end of November 1955. *Peter Sykes/ Online Transport Archive*

resulted in an unplanned extension to the system. The next service to be converted was that from the city centre to the University via Ardwick; the final trams operated on the route on 23 March 1940 to permit the new overhead to be erected with the trolleybus service commencing operation on 6 April 1940.

As a result of fuel shortages, it was decided to convert the motorbus route to Moston via Rochdale Road. Although the corporation had powers to replace tram with trolleybuses, these did not extend to the conversion of motorbus routes. Theoretically, new powers would need to be granted via a new Act; However, due to the war, permission was granted provided that the relevant powers were obtained eventually and retrospectively. The position was regularised for this and other wartime extensions over non-tram routes following the passage of the Manchester Corporation Act 1946, which received the Royal Assent on 26 July 1946. The route opened on 4 November 1940; this was followed on 9 December by the opening of the route from Denton to Haughton Green.

The Moston Lane service was extended to the Ben Brierley hotel early in 1941 and thence to Nuthurst Road on 14 July 1941; services from Stevenson Square to Nuthurst Road via

Alongside the twenty-eight two-axle trolleybuses supplied by Crossley, Manchester also acquired twelve three-axle TDD6s. Nos 1050-61 were fitted with the same manufacturer's sixty-eight-seat bodywork and were mainly allocated to Rochdale Road. Three-axle trolleybuses of this and the subsequent batch were never used on the Moston routes – where a number of corners (Thorp Road, Kenyon Road and the junction of Upper Conran Street with Moston Lane) were considered too sharp for the vehicles to negotiate safely – and rarely on the Guide Bridge and Haughton Green routes. No 1059, still retaining the streamlined livery that it had when new on its lower deck, is pictured here at Fallowfield on 22 September 1951 towards the end of its life; it was withdrawn later that month. All of the batch were taken out of service between July 1950 and April 1956. *R.L. Wilson/Online Transport Archive*

The second batch of three-axle trolleybuses delivered during 1938 were twenty-eight Leyland TTB4s – Nos 1062-87 – fitted with similar Crossley-built sixty-eight-seat bodywork to that supplied on Nos 1050-61. Here, on 10 April 1954, No 1079 is also seen turning into Portland with a service on route 218X. No 1079 was destined to be one of the last of the batch to be withdrawn; it and No 1074 survived until April 1956. The remainder of the type succumbed between June 1950 and March 1956. *R.L. Wilson/Online Transport Archive*

Oldham Road commenced on the same day with trolleybuses being allocated to Hyde Road depot for the first time simultaneously. There were plans – not executed – for an extension to serve the Blackley estate. On 2 August 1941, a further extension saw the service extended along Oldham Road a short distance beyond Nuthurst Road to a new terminus at Gardener's Arms. There was to be one further short extension beyond Gardener's Arms when the section to serve the A.V. Roe factory at Greengate opened on 23 August 1943. This was served at peak hours and represented the final wartime extension.

With peace restored in 1945, the corporation reconfirmed its policy of converting its remaining tram routes; there was one service – that along Hyde Road to Gee Cross – that had been slated for conversion to trolleybus operation before the war, but which had been deferred as a result of hostilities. The first post-war extensions saw the University service extended to Moss Lane East on 14 January 1946 and thence to Platt Lane on 20 February 1946; the section from Rochdale Road along Miller Street to Corporation Street, which became the city centre terminus of the Platt Lane route, opened on 12 July 1948.

The process of converting the route to Gee Cross commenced on 30 December 1947 when trams ceased to serve the section beyond the borough boundary at Broomstair Bridge to Gee Cross as a result of road repairs. On 14 March 1948, the tram service along

Hyde Road to Broomstair Bridge was replaced by a temporary bus service in order to facilitate the erection of the trolleybus service. Work completed, the new trolleybus service was introduced on 16 January 1950; it was destined to be the last extension to open. The total network now extended over some forty-four route miles, of which seventeen were outside the city boundaries.

By the early 1950s the future of the trolleybus system was under consideration. The general manager, A.F. Neal (who had replaced Pilcher following the latter's retirement in 1946), produced a report in 1952; this analysed the advantages and disadvantages of both trolleybuses and motorbuses and the cost of operation. Whether or not the trolleybus network was increased – and the report identified a number of routes that could be potentially converted to trolleybus operation – the report noted that the pre-war trolleybuses required replacement. On 29 April 1953, the conclusions of the report – that replacement vehicles be purchased but that consideration of new services be deferred – were accepted.

However, in September 1954, faced by the need to replace the overhead on the services to Moston and order further new trolleybuses in addition to the sixty-two ordered

Although delivered between April and September 1940, the thirty-seven Leyland TB5s ordered the previous year did not all immediately enter service; some were in store for some time and it was not until July and August 1941 that the last of the batch saw service. With the exception of Nos 1104 and 1133, which were latterly based at Hyde Road (and survived until 1959 – much later than the remainder of the type), all spent their operational career based at Rochdale Road and were used largely on the Moston routes. This batch was unusual in being the only trolleybuses received by Manchester between 1938 and 1950 not to be bodied by Crossley; the batch had fifty-four-seat bodies supplied by English Electric. With the exception of Nos 1104 and 1133, all were withdrawn between June 1954 and July 1956. *Roy Marshall/The Bus Archive*

The second batch of trolleybuses largely delivered during 1940 and 1941 – although the final five examples were not received until 1942 and 1943 – for the services introduced during 1940 were forty additional Crossley TDD4s – Nos 1137-176 – fitted with the same supplier's fifty-four-seat bodywork. On 1 March 1952, No 1151 is seen in Piccadilly prior to departure with a service on route 219X. Although the first of the batch to be withdrawn – No 1139 – was taken out service in August 1953, more than half remained operational at the start of 1959. All, however, had been withdrawn by the end of September 1960. *R.L. Wilson/Online Transport Archive*

pursuant to the 1953 policy, Neil advocated that the trolleybuses on these routes be replaced by motorbuses. The following month the proposals were accepted; the services to Gardener's Arms were converted in two stages on 24 April 1955 and 7 August 1955; the earlier date also saw Rochdale Road depot closed to trolleybuses, with all surviving trolleybuses then allocated to Hyde Road. City centre redevelopment resulted in the conversion of the Corporation Street to Platt Lane service on 31 May 1959. The next route to succumb was that to Haughton Green via Denton, which was last operated by trolleybuses on 4 July 1960; additional housing beyond the existing terminus would have required an extension to the route, which, given the circumstances, was unlikely to be approved as motorbuses offered greater flexibility.

The remaining services were mostly operated jointly with Ashton; there had been much discussion over the previous decade as to their future and, as a result (given Manchester's initial thoughts that the main services would survive until late in the 1960s) Ashton had acquired new trolleybuses in 1956 despite wanting to see a rapid conversion. On 6 December 1962, Manchester decided that the next conversion would be the service to Gee Cross – converted on 28 April 1963 (this was a gradual process that commenced

Above: **Appropriately seen** on route 210, the route for which the batch was purchased, is No 1200 the first of thirty-eight Crossley 'Empire' TDD42/1s fitted with Crossley fifty-eight-seat bodywork that were delivered during 1949 and 1950. These were the first trolleybuses that Manchester acquired post-war and were based at Hyde Road depot for their entire operational life. Primarily used on the 210, they were also used on other services. All were withdrawn between January and October 1963, with route 210 being converted to bus operation during April that year. *J. Joyce/Online Transport Archive*

Opposite above: **Delivered between** March and October 1951, Nos 1240-255 were Crossley 'Dominion' TDD64/1s fitted with Crossley-built sixty-six-seat bodywork. These sixteen vehicles were the only 'Dominion' type constructed and were largely designed for operation for peak hour duties and short workings on routes 210, 213X and 218X. Pictured on 28 October 1961 heading inbound towards Piccadilly on a 210X working is No 1250; following the withdrawal of the entire batch between January and July 1963, No 1250 was secured for preservation. *R.L. Wilson/Online Transport Archive*

Opposite below: The last new trolleybuses purchased by Manchester were sixty-two BUT 9621Ts that were delivered during 1955. Although badged as BUTs, the chassis of the vehicles were in fact manufactured at the old Crossley works at Errwood Park, Crossley having been taken over by AEC (one of the partners with Leyland in BUT) in 1951 and were in fact the last chassis to be constructed at the factory. All were fitted with sixty-seat bodywork supplied by Burlingham with No 1302 – seen here at Stalybridge in June 1964 – being delivered first for testing. Destined for a relatively short life in Manchester, all were withdrawn between the summer of 1964 and the end of trolleybus operation in December 1966. *Harry Luff/Online Transport Archive*

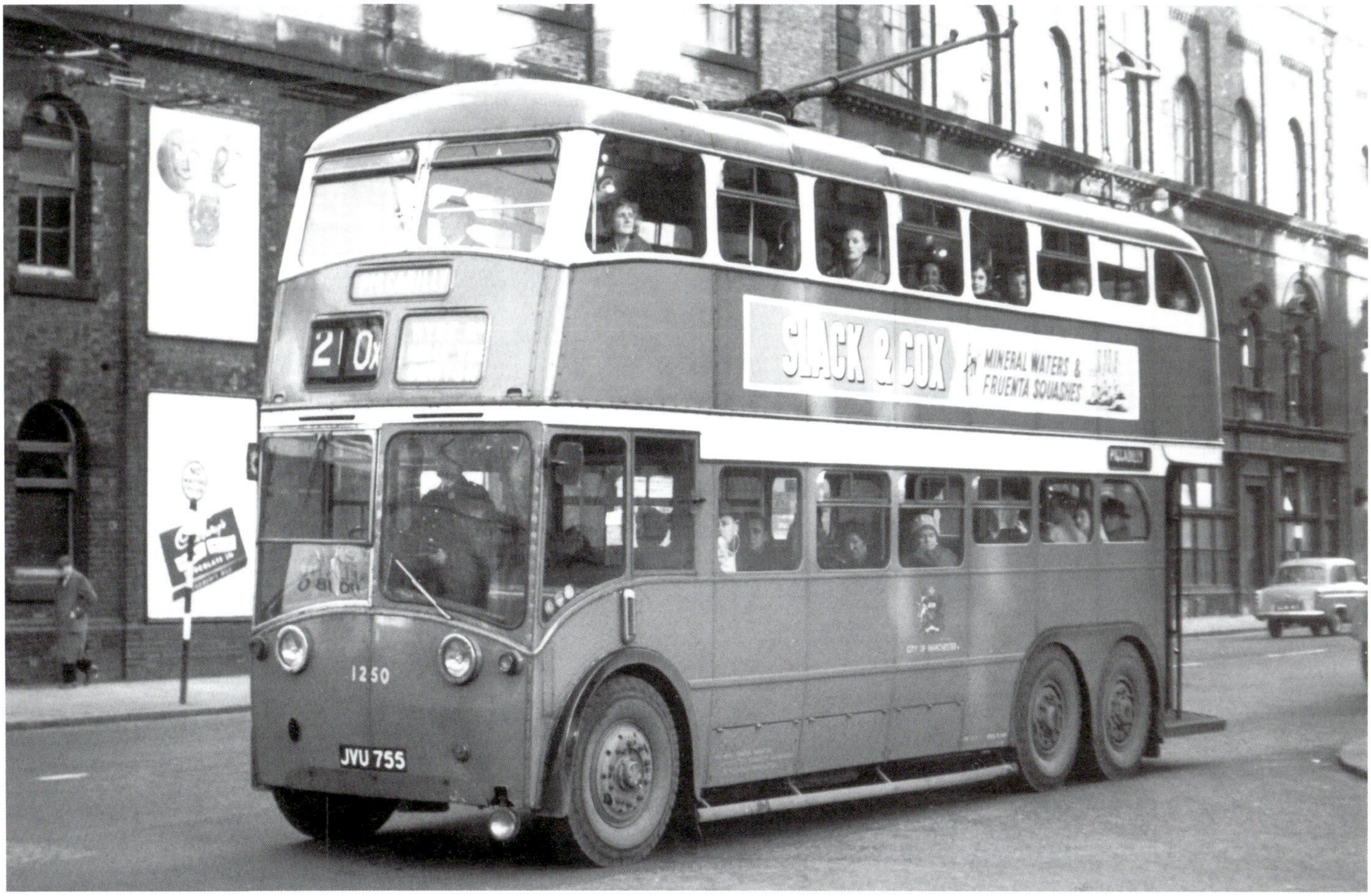
SLACK & COX
MINERAL WATERS &
FRUENTA SQUASHES
1250
JVU 755

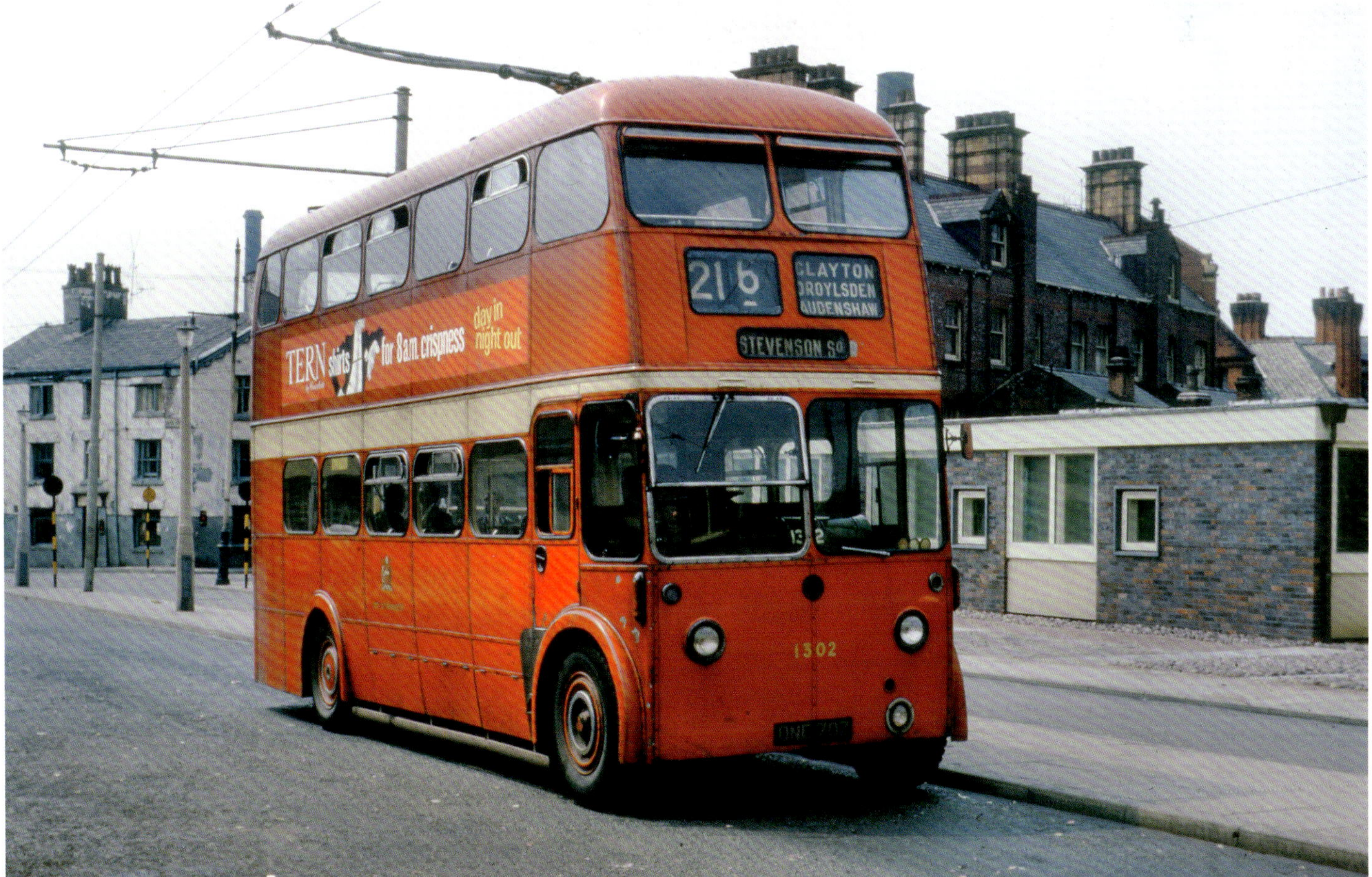
CLAYTON
DROYLSDEN
AUDENSHAW
STEVENSON Sq
TERN shirts for 8a.m. crispness
day in night out
1302

On 31 December 1966 – the day after it had performed as Manchester's official last trolleybus – No 1344 had one final duty when it, alongside preserved ex-Rotherham No 44, undertook a farewell tour of the system for enthusiasts. Here, No 1344 is seen, still bearing its commemorative messages, alongside No 44 in Stevenson Square as passengers board for this one final trip. Following these duties, No 1344 was preserved, the only one of the batch to survive. *R.L. Wilson/Online Transport Archive*

in January 1963) – leaving the majority of joint services until 1967. The next service to succumb – somewhat unexpectedly with no prior notice – was that to Ashton via Guide Bridge; this last operated on 10 October 1964.

This left the original joint services along Ashton Old Road and Ashton New Road operational; on 1 May 1966, Manchester ceased to provide trolleybuses on the Ashton Old Road routes, replacing them with motorbuses, although Ashton continued to operate duties on it until the final day of trolleybus operation – 30 December 1966 – when the last services from Manchester to Ashton were provided by two of the Ashton fleet (No 83 providing additional accommodation to No 87) whilst the last Manchester vehicles to operate were Nos 1302, 1353 and 1354; the last of these was destined to be the last Manchester trolleybus in public service.

This was not quite the end of the system as the following day, two trolleybuses – Manchester No 1344 (which had already been acquired for preservation) and preserved Rotherham No 44 – made a farewell tour of the system. Alongside No 1344, No 1250 was also secured for preservation; these are now based at Sandtoft and Boyle Street respectively.

Fleet number	Registration	Chassis	Body	New	Withdrawn	Notes
1000-027	DXJ951-978	Crossley TDD4	Crossley H54R	1938	1953-56	Built using MCCW frames
1028-037	DXJ979-988	Leyland TB4	Crossley H58R	1938	1951-55	Built using MCCW frames
1050-061	DXJ989-993/ ENB175-181	Crossley TDD6	Crossley H68R	1938	1950-56	Built using MCCW frames
1062-087	ENB182-207	Leyland TTB4	Crossley H68R	1938	1950-56	Built using MCCW frames
1100-136	GNA18-54	Leyland TB5	EE H54R	1940-41	1954-59	
1137-176	GNA55-94	Crossley TDD4	Crossley H54R	1940	1953-60	Built using MCCW frames
1200-237	JVU707-744	Crossley Empire	Crossley H58R	1949-50	1963	
1240-255	JVU745-760	Crossley Dominion	Crossley H66R	1951	1963	1250 preserved
1301-347	ONE701-747	BUT 9612T	Burlingham H60R	1955	1962-66	1344 preserved
1348-362	ONE748-762	BUT 9612T	Burlingham H60R	1956	1964-66	

Route number	From	To	Date Opened	Date Closed	Notes
37 (36X from August 1941 as a short working of 36; 36X dropped July 1948)	Stevenson Square	Nuthurst Road (via Oldham Road)	14 July 1941	7 August 1955	Route ceased August 1955; short working 36X rarely operated post 12 July 1948 and route number not used
26 (216 from April 1950)	Stevenson Square	Stalybridge (via Ashton New Road)	31 July 1938	30 December 1966	Terminus relocated in Stalybridge November 1959
57 (17 from July 1947 and 217 from April 1950)	Ashton	Denton	1 July 1940	4 July 1960	
57 (17 from July 1947 and 217 from April 1950)	Denton	Haughton Green	9 December 1940	4 July 1960	
30 (213 from April 1952)	Rochdale Road	University	6 April 1940	31 May 1959	
30 (213 from April 1952)	University	Moss Lane East	14 January 1946	31 May 1959	
30 (213 from April 1952)	Moss Lane East	Platt Lane	20 February 1946	31 May 1959	
30 (213 from April 1952)	Rochdale Road	Corporation Street	12 July 1948	31 May 1959	

Route number	From	To	Date Opened	Date Closed	Notes
55 (Moston Lane short working 60X following extension of 55 to Ben Brierley 1941 and 33X on opening of extension to Gardener's Arms August 1941; some morning workings of 33X showed 34 between 1949 and 1953; became 214 August 1953)	Stevenson Square	Moston Lane (via Rochdale Road)	4 November 1940	23 April 1955	Terminus transferred to Church Street during summer of 1941
55 (short working to Ben Brierley became 33 on opening of extension to Gardener's Arms August 1941; 33 became 212X August 1953)	Moston Lane	Ben Brierley	Early 1941	24 April 1955	Covered section on Conran Street, Upper Conran Street and Moston Lane
55 (short working to Nuthurst Road became 32X on opening of extension to Gardener's Arms August 1941)	Ben Brierley	Nuthurst Road	14 July 1941	24 April 1955	Route 32X ceased to operate by early 1950s
32 (became 212 August 1953)	Nuthurst Road	Gardener's Arms	2 August 1941	24 April 1955	
32 (became 212 August 1953)	Gardeners Arms	Greengate (A. V. Roe factory)	23 August 1943	24 April 1955	Peak hours only
27 (27X short working to Edge Lane; became 215 and 215X in April 1950)	Stevenson Square	Audenshaw (Snipe Inn)	31 July 1938	30 December 1966	Cut back to Ryecroft Hall 24 May 1959
37 (36 from August 1941 with short working to Ben Brierley 37; became 31 in July 1948 when 37 became 31X; renumbered 211 and 211X respectively in August 1953)	Nuthurst Road	Gardener's Arms	2 August 1941	7 August 1955	

Route number	From	To	Date Opened	Date Closed	Notes
210	George Street	Gee Cross	16 January 1950	28 April 1963	City terminus transferred to Piccadilly 1956
28 (short workings to The Trough [29] and Fairfield Road [29X] introduced 21 March 1938 and to Snipe [28X] on 31 July 1938; 29 and 29X became 31 and 31X in October 1939; 31/31X absorbed into 29X and 29X became short working on route 29 July 1948; 28/28X became 218 and 218X in April 1950)	Piccadilly	Stalybridge (via Ashton Old Road)	1 March 1938	30 December 1966	Terminus relocated in Stalybridge November 1959; last operated by Manchester trolleybus on 1 May 1966; operated by Ashton Corporation trolleybuses and Manchester buses until 30 December.
29 (former routes 31 and 31X became short working 29X July 1948; 29/29X became 219 and 219X in April 1950)	Piccadilly	Guide Bridge (via Ashton Old Road)	16 October 1939	10 October 1964	On 17 June 1957 certain short workings to The Trough on 29X were diverted to start from Aytoun Street and redesignated 212; service ceased 2 November 1963
29 (former routes 31 and 31X became short working 29X July 1948; 29/29X became 219 and 219X in April 1950)	Guide Bridge	Ashton	22 March 1940	10 October 1964	

On 13 August 1950 No 1202 is seen in Piccadilly with a service on route 210 towards Hyde. One of the Crossley Empire TDD42/1s delivered during 1949 and 1950, No 1202 entered service in May 1959 and survived until June 1963. Two of the batch – Nos 1201 and 1204 – were equipped with automatic acceleration equipment from new with the remainder being fitted with the equipment retrospectively, No 1202 in March 1952. *Peter N. Williams/Online Transport Archive*

NEWCASTLE UPON TYNE

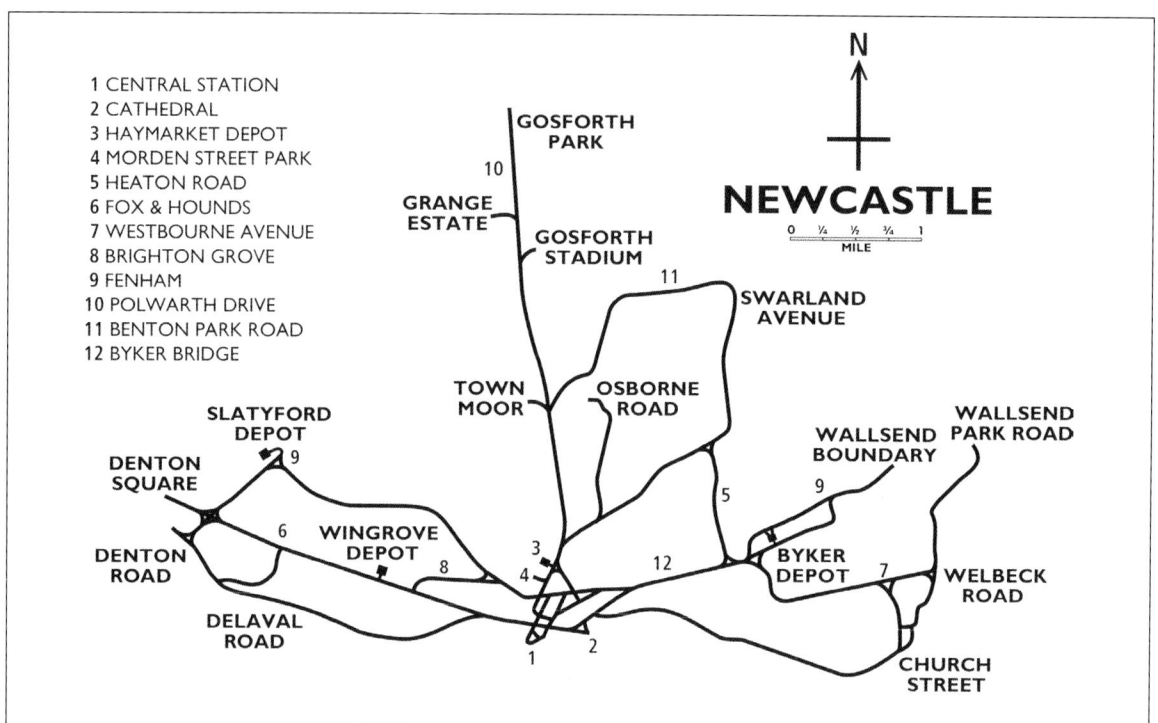

Newcastle upon Tyne possessed a significant standard gauge electric tramway; at its peak this extended to some fifty-one route miles but was closely integrated with the BET-owned Gateshead & District Tramways Co following the opening of the first of two physical connections between the two systems in 1923. Over the succeeding decades, the development of public transport was determined by the often-differing policies of the company and the corporation.

By the late 1920s, despite having spent £686,000 upgrading its tramway since the end of the First World War, Newcastle Corporation was uncertain as to the future. As elsewhere, significant track replacement work was required and much of the fleet was increasingly aged, despite the purchase of more than seventy new trams between 1918 and 1926. In late 1931, after much debate, it was agreed that the tramway track must be patched up. This was not, however, a long-term solution and, in 1934, attention again turned to the possible conversion of the system and, on 8 May 1934, the corporation decided to seek powers for the operation of trolleybuses; these were quickly obtained for the Wallsend to Denton Burn route through the Newcastle upon Tyne Corporation Act 1934, which received the Royal Assent on 31 July 1934. These powers were further strengthened by a second Act – the Newcastle upon Tyne Corporation (General Powers) Act 1935 – which received the Royal Assent on 2 August 1935.

Between 1935 and 1940, Newcastle Corporation acquired 113 new trolleybuses; with the exception of one Daimler, No 112, the remainder came from three suppliers – AEC, Guy and Karrier – with the majority receiving bodywork supplied by Metro-Cammell. A total of thirty-five Guy BTXs – such as No 105 illustrated here – were acquired; all of these bar two received Metro-Cammell bodies, the exceptions – Nos 78 and 109 – had bodywork by Roe and Northern Coachbuilders respectively. All of the pre-war trolleybuses had two staircases and front-exit doors; all had 300 added to their original fleet number during 1946 and all were withdrawn during 1949 and 1950 as the post-war BUTs and Sunbeams were delivered; No 105, by now renumbered 405, was taken out of service during 1949. *W.J. Haynes*

During 1935, work proceeded on the installation of the overhead and the acquisition of the initial batch of trolleybuses. Following official inspection on 23 and 24 September 1935, the first new trolleybus service – linking Wallsend (Park Road) with Denton Burn (extending beyond the original tram terminus on the West Road and turning in a loop from Fox & Hounds to Denton Road and back to West Road) – was officially inaugurated on 1 October 1935 with public services commencing on the 9½-mile route on the following day. The new trolleybuses were allocated to Wingrove Depot, which was shared with trams. The new service was a success and required additional trolleybuses to be ordered; pending the delivery of these, temporary sanction was given to supplement the trolleybus service with motorbuses. Interestingly, that part of the new route from the city centre to the Denton Burn loop had since 1929 been operated by motor buses (running alongside the trams on Westgate Road to termini across the city in Heaton and Walker) and that service was cut back to run from the Central Station with the arrival of the trolleybuses.

Further route conversions and extensions were approved; these were authorised by Royal Assent being granted on 25 March 1937 to the Newcastle upon Tyne (Trolley

74 • BRITISH TROLLEYBUS SYSTEMS – LANCASHIRE, NORTHERN IRELAND, SCOTLAND AND NORTHERN ENGLAND

During the late 1930s, Newcastle took delivery of a number of Karrier E6As fitted with Metro-Cammell sixty-seat bodywork; typical of these is No 387, which is seen here on Neville Street during 1949 with passengers boarding prior to heading towards Fox & Hounds with a service on route 34 (this route number was a relatively recent change dating from 1 November 1948). Delivered as No 87 and entering service in August 1938, this was one of fourteen of the type to enter service during that year. Nos 85-98 were renumbered in 1946 and all were withdrawn during 1949 as the post-war deliveries allowed the older trolleybuses to be replaced. *C. Carter/Online Transport Archive*

For the expansion of the system post-war, as part of the programme to eliminate the final trams, a significant number of new vehicles were acquired during 1948 and 1949. All had a rear platform and single staircase configuration, very different from the design of the pre-war fleet. The second batch delivered – albeit the first numerically – of the post-war deliveries were thirty-six Sunbeams F4s fitted with MCCW fifty-six-seat bodywork. Nos 443-78 entered service between November 1948 and March 1949 with No 468 being displayed at the 1948 Commercial Motor Show. Here No 477 is pictured heading to Denton Square with a service on route 34B. This was one of a number of routes converted to bus operation on 2 June 1963. All of this batch of vehicles – known to the crews as 'Doodlebugs' (as were all subsequent two-axle trolleybuses) – were all withdrawn between June 1961 and the end of May 1963. *Harry Luff/Online Transport Archive*

Vehicles) Order Confirmation Act 1937 and on 29 July 1938 to the Newcastle upon Tyne (Trolley Vehicles) Order Confirmation Act 1938.

As a result, on 19 September 1937 trolleybuses replaced trams on the service from Brighton Grove to two termini in Walker (Church Street and Welbeck Road). As part of this conversion, trolleybuses began operation from the main car sheds at Byker for the first time. The trolleybus fleet by now numbered 67 vehicles. On 24 April 1938, after the trolleybus wiring on the West Road had been extended to the new city boundary at Denton Square, some of the journeys on the Walker to Brighton Grove and Wallsend Park Road to Denton Burn routes ran to the new terminus.

Three further tram routes were converted during 1938. The first of these – on 1 August 1938 – saw trolleybuses take over the service from the Central Station to Fenham (Ovington Grove terminus, just beyond Two Ball Lonnen). The remainder of the Westerhope tram route beyond the new trolleybus terminus was abandoned at this time. For several years it had been operating on Saturdays only to handle weekend shopping traffic, the main service having been replaced by motorbuses during 1929. A short spur southwards from the Westerhope tramway to Denton Burn had closed, because of poor patronage, in August 1928 after just 2½ years in operation. The next tram services replaced – on 2 September 1938 – were those to Osborne Road and to Wallsend Boundary

During 1948, Newcastle took delivery of twenty 8ft 0in wide BUT 9641Ts fitted with MCCW seventy-seat bodywork; Nos 479-98 had originally been ordered by London Transport as part of the order for the 'Q1' class but, following agreement with the Ministry of Transport and the manufacturers, had been diverted to Tyneside. As a consequence of their provenance, the vehicles had a number of features common with the LPTB-supplied batch; this included London pattern large destination boxes. These were modified by being partially blanked off by black paint as evinced by No 491, which is seen at the Gosforth Park terminus of route 31. This service, which commenced operation in place of the trams, on 18 April 1948 was to survive until conversion to bus operation on 1 February 1964. Nicknamed the 'Gosforth Trolleys', all bar one – No 495 – lived on until withdrawn en bloc at the end of May 1965, having survived the Gosforth routes by 12 months. *Phil Tatt/Online Transport Archive*

on Shields Road, both also running from the Central Station. Trolleybuses for the Osborne Road route were stabled at Haymarket Depot, for the first time. By the end of 1938 the trolleybus fleet numbered 101 vehicles. When the Westmorland Road tram route was next converted in July 1939, however, it was replaced not by trolleybuses but by combining, at much lower cost, four existing motor bus routes, two of them being the shortened services from Heaton and Walker that had been cut back to the Central Station from Denton Burn when the first trolleybuses started running in 1935. The other two were the feeder services introduced in 1936 from Caroline Pit on Slatyford Lane and the Morris Works in Cowgate to the Westmorland Road tram terminus.

In early 1939, plans were developed for the conversion of virtually the entire remaining tram system to trolleybus operation; the next conversion planned was the service to Elswick Road. However, the declaration of war in September 1939 put all the plans into abeyance and ensured that the surviving tram routes had a longer life than might have been anticipated. Nevertheless, the corporation acquired, in the Newcastle-upon-Tyne (Trolley Vehicles) Order Confirmation Act 1940 (17 July), powers for replacement of the Elswick Road tram service by trolleybuses. As events proved, it was not until June 1944 that the conversion actually took place, when sanction was given for capital expenditure and additional new vehicles. Ironically, in spite of the general wartime constraints on vehicle deliveries, the twelve additional trolleybuses ordered in 1939 to meet increasing service requirements were still released to the corporation, eventually arriving during 1940 and bringing the number of trolleybuses in the fleet to 113.

In March 1941 the general manager, Thomas P. Easton, retired, to be replaced by Harold Citford Godsmark, who had previously been general manager at Huddersfield (and who had overseen the considerable expansion of the trolleybus network there in

Pictured outside Central station is No 524; this was one of a batch – nicknamed 'Coffins' because they were long and thin – of thirty vehicles, Nos 499-528, that were new in late 1948. Sunbeam supplied the chassis – the company's new S7 model – and the vehicles were fitted with 70-seat bodies supplied by Northern Coachbuilders, a local company. One of the batch – No 512 – was displayed at the Commercial Motor Show of 1948. The majority of the batch survived until the end of May 1965 when the last twenty-three were taken out of service; No 501 was preserved on withdrawal and is now in operation at Beamish Museum. *Ian Dunnet/Online Transport Archive*

the immediate pre-war years). The new manager confirmed that the corporation's policy remained conversion to trolleybus operation after the war.

On 30 June 1941, the existing service from Wallsend Boundary via Shields Road to the Central Station was converted to a cross-city route westwards via Westgate Road, Fox & Hounds and part of the Denton Burn loop through Old Benwell to a new terminus erected on Denton Road. At the same time, the service from St Nicholas' Cathedral ceased to use the Denton Burn loop for turning, running through to Denton Square instead. The Wallsend Park Road and Walker services continued to turn at Fox & Hounds as before. The short stretch of the loop between the new Denton Road Terminus and the West Road no longer carried a regular service of trolleybuses, just the motor bus service that ran from Caroline Pit to the city via Westmorland Road. There followed on 23 November 1941 an extension of the Fenham route from Ovington Grove to Bingfield Gardens; this ran along the route of the erstwhile tramway to Slatyford and Westerhope.

In order to supplement the fleet further to cope with growing wartime traffic, five vehicles were hired from Brighton Corporation for a brief period during 1942, replaced very quickly by nine trolleybuses hired from Bournemouth. Ten second-hand trolleybuses were purchased from Bradford at the end of that year, six of which entered service in early 1943 in wartime grey livery. Five of the Bournemouth vehicles remained in Newcastle until the end of the war, the others moving quickly away during 1943, three to South Shields for a short while.

The Elswick Road tramway conversion was finally completed on 11 June 1944; the new service continued to run via Clayton Street to a terminal point adjacent to Eldon Square called 'Monument' but was extended westward beyond the original tram terminus at the junction of Benwell Lane and Delaval Road to the new trolleybus terminus on Denton Road that had been constructed in 1941. This opening was facilitated by the delivery of the first twelve of the eighteen Karrier W4 utility trolleybuses allocated to Newcastle.

As the war progressed and as peace approached, the future of the tramways on both sides of the Tyne came under consideration. The operation of both systems was heavily interlinked, with almost all of the Gateshead & District Tramways company's services crossing the river into Newcastle. Corporation and company cars operated side-by-side on most routes. A comprehensive agreement was set up between the operators to control the number of cars in service, mileages operated and apportionment of fares revenue. The position south of the river was complicated by the fact that, under the terms of the 1870 Tramways Act, Gateshead Corporation had the right to purchase the tramway. Relations before the Second World War between the corporation and company – particularly over the possibility of tramcar replacement – had not been harmonious. On 29 July 1938, Royal Assent had been granted to the Gateshead and District Tramways and Trolley Vehicles Act 1938. This act, promoted by the company, empowered it to convert its tramway system to trolleybus operation but, by the outbreak of war in September 1939, no progress had been made. During 1944 and 1945, inconclusive negotiations were held but the possibility of conversion to trolleybus operation still remained in place. In the event, uncertainty about the future of the operation, given that nationalisation of the bus industry was looming on the horizon, led the company to decide upon the much less capital-intensive option of motorbuses instead of trolleybuses for tram replacements. Powers to achieve the conversion were enshrined in the Gateshead & District Tramways Act 1950, which received the Royal Assent on 12 July 1950. The process of tram to bus conversion in Gateshead began a little earlier, in March 1950, before the new Act actually took effect and using existing powers to operate motorbuses over the Gateshead tramways in the interim. From that date, Newcastle Corporation ceased to operate trams and thereafter the remaining cross-river tram services were operated solely by the

Above: **The final** Sunbeam trolleybuses acquired by Newcastle were twenty-five two-axle S4s fitted with Northern Coachbuilders fifty-six-seat bodywork. Nos 529-553 were new between December 1949 and March 1950; these were again purchased to permit the withdrawal of pre-war and wartime vehicles. No 541 is seen here on route 41 – a service that was introduced on 16 January 1949 as a circular service to Heaton Road (it operated in one direction; service 42 operated the other). Nos 529-553 were withdrawn in two batches in May 1963 and February 1964; No 541 was one of those taken out of service in the former. *Harry Luff/Online Transport Archive*

Opposite above: **On 5 March** 1950, No 575 is seen turning at Central Station with a circular service towards Benton Park Road. When recorded here, No 575 was virtually brand new having entered service in August 1949; it was one of a batch of twenty-five BUT 9611Ts – Nos 554-78 – with Northern Coachbuilders fifty-six-seat bodywork. The entire batch was withdrawn in early February 1964 following the conversion of routes 31, 37, 38, 39 and 40 on the first of that month. *John Meredith/Online Transport Archive*

Opposite below: **In 1950** a further batch of fifty BUT 9641Ts – No 579-628 – were acquired; again fitted with a seventy-seat Metro-Cammell body, these vehicles were virtually identical to the batch delivered during 1948 although there were many detail differences. The most obvious was, perhaps, the use of the standard Newcastle destination display – as evinced here by No 623 with a service on route 44 towards Fenham via Barrack Road – rather than the London-type display of the earlier batch. No 628 was displayed at the 1950 Commercial Motor Show and was used as a demonstrator at Tees-side during its journey to Tyneside. These fifty vehicles were to be the last trolleybuses to enter service with Newcastle and all were to be withdrawn between May 1965 and the final conversion of the system on 1 October 1966. No 623 was to see exactly sixteen years' service; it commenced operation on 1 October 1950 and was one of those that survived to the bitter end. Autospares, the Bingley-based scrap merchant, had agreed to purchase all of the remaining trolleybuses, and agreement was reached that resulted in the preservation of No 628. It now resides at the East Anglia Transport Museum at Carlton Colvile. *Jim Jordan/Online Transport Archive*

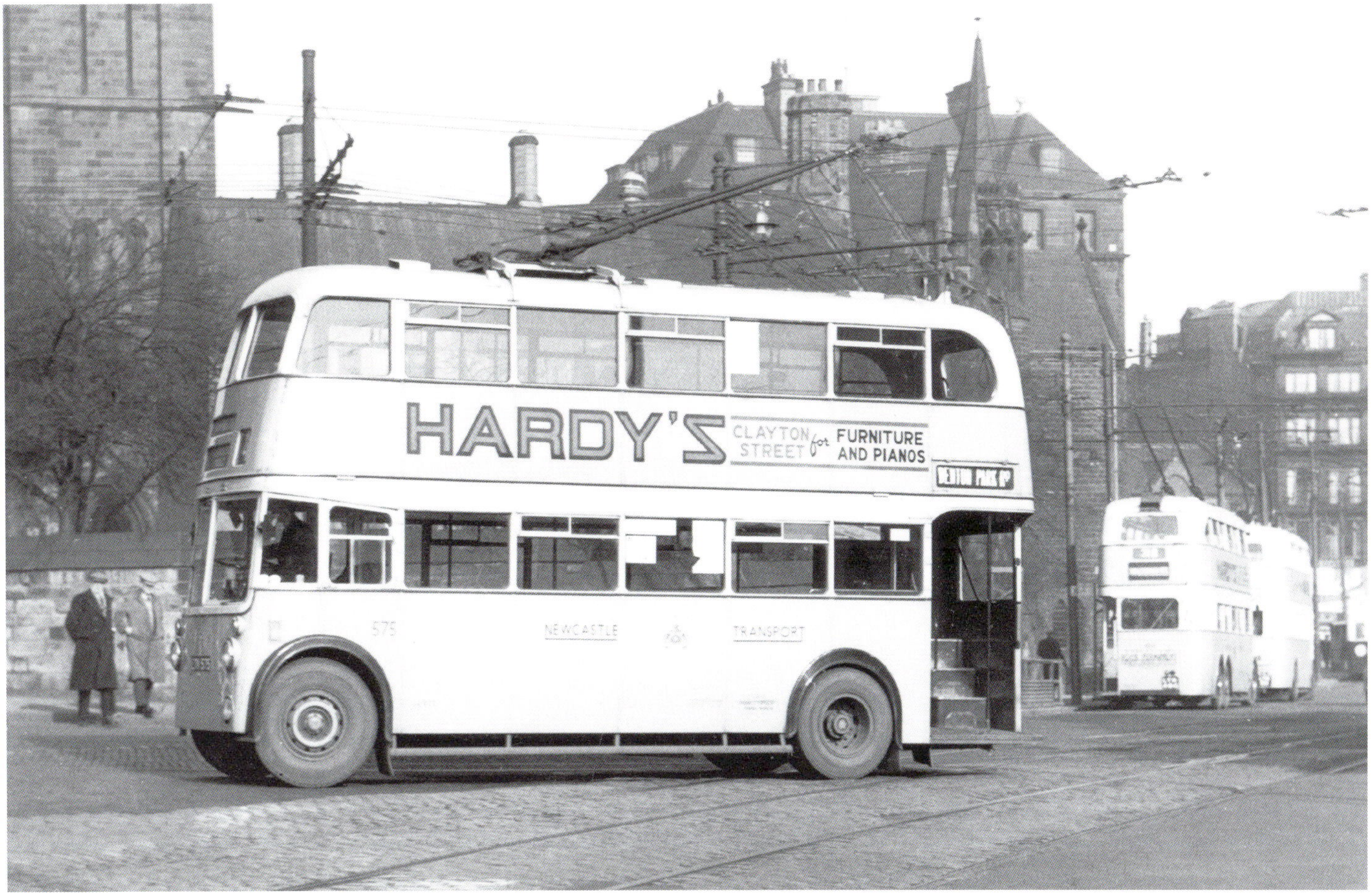
HARDY'S
CLAYTON STREET for FURNITURE AND PIANOS
575
NEWCASTLE
TRANSPORT

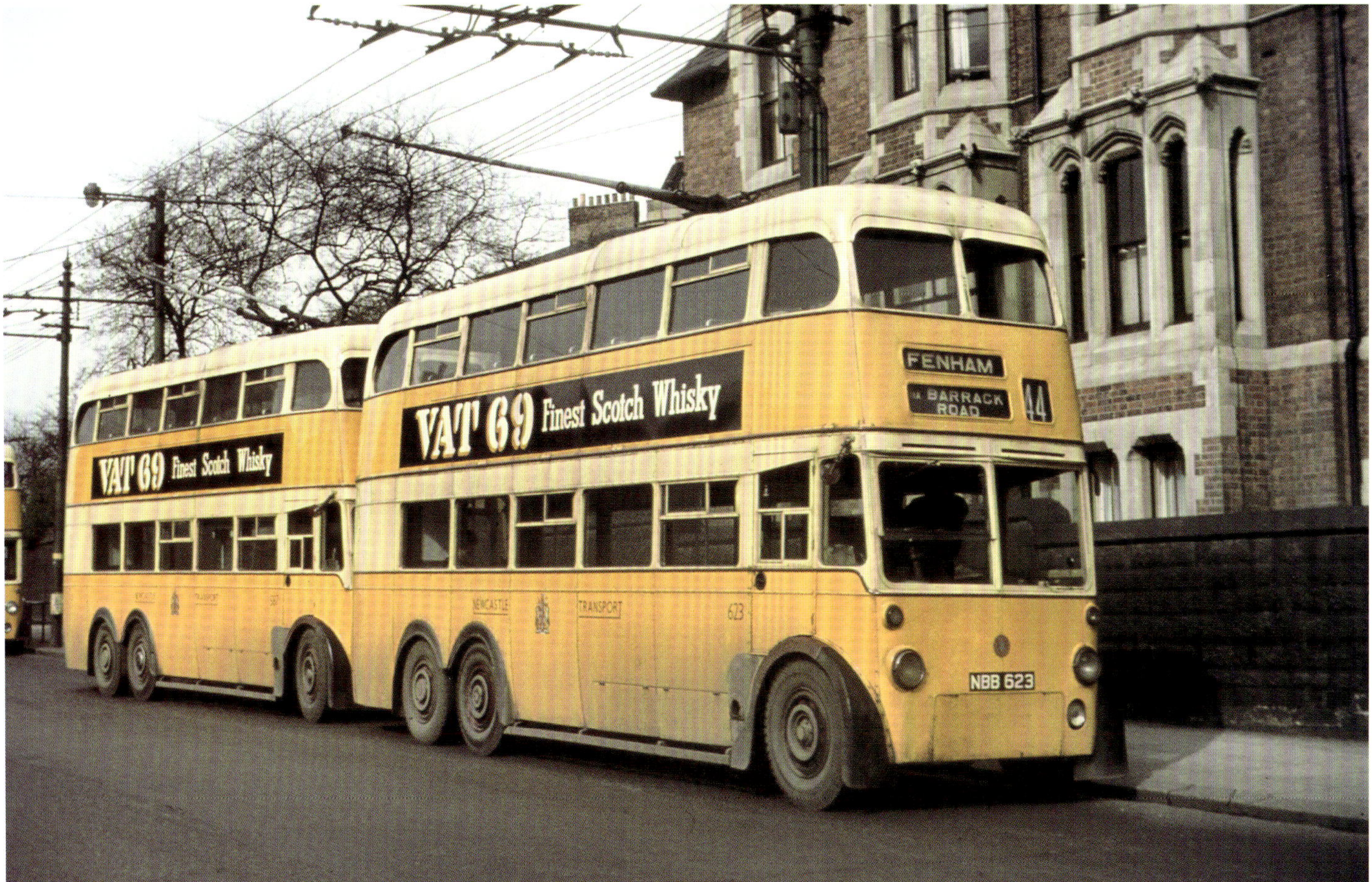
VAT 69 Finest Scotch Whisky
FENHAM
BARRACK ROAD
44
NEWCASTLE
TRANSPORT
623
NBB 623
VAT 69 Finest Scotch Whisky

Gateshead company, until their final withdrawal in stages between March and August 1951, resulting in the ironic consequence that the last trams in Newcastle were those operated by the company almost eighteen months after the last corporation tram had run. As had been the case with the trams, the Gateshead company's new motorbus services were operated jointly with the corporation, crossing the river by both the High Level and Tyne Bridges.

In preparation for the ultimate abandonment of tram operation in Newcastle and conversion to trolleybus operation, the corporation had acquired the necessary additional powers courtesy of the Newcastle upon Tyne Corporation (Trolley Vehicles) Order Confirmation Act 1945 (31 October) and the Newcastle upon Tyne Corporation Act 1946, which received the Royal Assent on 12 July 1946. It was reported in *Commercial Motor* in December 1945, 'As soon as opportunity occurs, the Corporation of Newcastle-upon-Tyne has decided that its trams shall be displaced by trolleybuses.' However, what followed was not at all in accordance with that plan...

First, in June 1946, the Throckley tram route was converted to single-deck motorbus operation and not to trolleybuses. Admittedly, this was a special case, caused by the corporation's commitment to run the replacement service through Lemington centre itself, passing over two weak railway bridges that had caused trams to be re-routed away from the village within a few years of opening in 1915. Only single-deck motorbuses were light enough to pass over those bridges.

The Gateshead company's change of conversion strategy, previously described, left the corporation with no option but to follow suit with motorbus conversion for the tramway services it operated jointly with the company. In addition, the corporation was reflecting on the need not just to replace tram services 'as-is' but also to meet demand from the post-war housing developments in the outskirts of the city, and beyond. The inherent flexibility of motorbus operation, coupled with the much lower capital cost when developing new services on routes where trams had not previously operated, was also a key factor. Finally, the low level of new trolleybus production immediately after the war was an unexpected factor that contributed to the change of strategy by the corporation. As a result, between 1946 and March 1950, as the corporation steadily reduced its involvement with tramways, several routes were converted to motorbus instead of trolleybus operation.

On 30 November 1947 the Elswick Road to Monument and Central Station to Osborne Road trolleybus services were combined to form a new through route from Denton Road to Osborne Road. The Monument terminus was thereafter served only by peak hour services. On the same date the Pilgrim Street to Westbourne Avenue service was extended westward to run along Elswick Road to Delaval Road.

The last Gosforth Park trams operated on 16 April 1948 with trolleybuses taking over two days later in what was the first major post-War conversion of tramway to trolleybus in accordance with the original strategy. On the same date, the Gateshead trams that had shared the North Road service with the corporation as far as Henry Street terminus in Gosforth were diverted to the Central Station. Although extension of the trolleybus route beyond the Park entrance – to replace the tramway through to Benton via the Gosforth Park Light Railway and West Moor – was sanctioned in the 1946 Act it was, like a number of other authorised routes, never completed. The next conversion, of the West Moor tram route along with the branch to Forest Hall, took place on 31 October 1948. Motorbuses were introduced on these routes, the outer parts of which lay outside the city boundary. Associated trolleybus services commenced the following day, running inside the boundary on the Benton loop, from Town Moor on the Gosforth route via Benton Park Road (passing the terminus circle at Swarland Avenue) to connect with the existing Osborne Road route on Jesmond Road. This was followed on 16 January 1949 by the section along Heaton Road to create a further circular route via Byker Bridge and Jesmond Road.

On 10 September 1949, Newcastle trams operated for the last time on the Scotswood Bridge route; these were replaced by motorbus services that ran across the city to destinations in parts of the east where trolleybus conversion did not take place. Tramway operation in the city was now restricted to the sections from the city centre to the two bridges across the Tyne over which the joint services operated; corporation trams continued to operate over these routes until 4 March 1950 when all tram services over the Tyne Bridge ceased operation. As already noted, the last trams operated on Tyneside in August 1951 when the Gateshead tramway services over the High Level Bridge were finally withdrawn.

The new trolleybus extensions by the corporation were facilitated by the introduction of 186 new trolleybuses between 1948 and 1950; these arrivals also permitted the withdrawal of all of the pre-war trolleybus fleet with the wartime deliveries being put into store. The system now extended over thirty-five route miles.

It is of note that in the period between 1945 and 1950, Newcastle Corporation also put into service 245 additional motorbuses. All these new arrivals meant that, as well as the whole pre-war trolleybus fleet being replaced, all but fourteen of the pre-war motorbuses and the two hundred or so trams still in operation at the end of the Second World War were withdrawn from service.

The next extension to the Newcastle trolleybus system – on 28 October 1951 – saw wires erected along Broadway West in Gosforth to serve new housing on the Grange Estate. Although further powers were granted in the Newcastle upon Tyne Corporation Act 1952, which received the Royal Assent on 1 August 1952, for trolleybus services to Westerhope and an extension of the new Grange Estate route, these were not acted on. From 1 August 1955, the Wallsend to Denton Burn service was revised so that all services from Wallsend and Walker ran through to Denton Square, the Fox & Hounds reversing point then being used only for peak-hour services.

The final major extension – linked to the opening of the new Slatyford Lane Depot (on 10 July 1956, replacing Wingrove Depot) – saw services introduced to the newly wired section along Silver Lonnen between the existing terminus at Bingfield Gardens and the West Road at Denton Burn; this had previously been part of the Denton Burn tram route that closed in 1928. Newcastle's longest trolleybus service (at just under ten miles) was then introduced, running in a route the shape of which is best described as a 'lower-case d', from Osborne Road, through the city centre and along Elswick Road to Denton Road, then via Silver Lonnen to Fenham and back to the city to terminate at the Central Station. During 1957 a diversion route east of Byker Depot was erected to permit operation of trolleybuses to and from Wallsend Boundary via the Fossway and Coutts Road should the main route along Shields Road be blocked by heavy rail movements between the C.A. Parsons factories on both sides of that thoroughfare. Parsons met the expense of the diversion route.

At the end of 1957, Haymarket Depot was closed and the site sold to King's College (later to be re-titled University of Newcastle upon Tyne), who demolished the buildings and erected a new Physics department in their place. A commercial vehicle parking area in nearby Morden Street was converted into a motor and trolleybus parking facility and used to stable vehicles between the morning and evening peaks. Depot office facilities were provided in the Handysides Arcade.

In December 1962 the general manager, Frank S. Taylor, produced a report recommending the conversion of the trolleybus system to motorbus operation; this was to become official corporation policy early in 1963. The reasons were similar to those espoused elsewhere – road reconstruction, lack of flexibility in operation, high cost of infrastructure renewal, etc. – and the Manager was clearly a believer in the motorbus. He was quoted in *Commercial Motor* during 1964 praising 'the Atlantean buses introduced two years ago, and to be used eventually on all routes. Mr. Taylor said the vehicles were easier and cheaper to maintain than the smaller buses and trolley vehicles used hitherto; and there were fewer platform accidents.' The conversion of the system – which now extended over almost 36½ route miles – was completed in three years, by the end of 1966, rather than by 1968 as originally anticipated.

Effectively the system succumbed in four stages. The first – on 2 June 1963 – saw the conversion of the very first route from Denton Square to Wallsend. This was followed on 1 February 1964 by the final operation of trolleybuses on the routes to Gosforth Park, Grange Estate, the Benton Park Road circular and the two cross-city services from Denton Road to Swarland Avenue. The penultimate stage – on 29 May 1965 – featured the Fenham, Osborne Road, Wallsend Boundary and most of the Elswick Road services. This left only the routes serving Brighton Grove, Denton Square, Elswick Road and Walker in operation. After partial rerouting in August 1965, brought about by the closure for redevelopment of Church Street, these last services finally closed on 1 October 1966, exactly thirty-one years to the day after the system came into being. There was no official ceremony, with No 599 being the last trolleybus in service. Of the fleet, only two examples – Nos 501 and 628, normally based at Beamish Museum and the East Anglia Transport Museum at Carlton Colville respectively – survive in preservation.

Fleet number	Registration	Chassis	Body	New	Withdrawn	Notes
10-14 (renumbered 310-14 1946)	BVK800-804	AEC 664T	EE H60D	1935	1949-50	
15-19 (renumbered 315-19 1946)	BVK805-809	AEC 664T	Brush H60D	1935	1948-50	
20-29 (renumbered	BVK810-819	Karrier E6A	MCCW H60D	1935	1949-50	
30-39 (renumbered 330-39 1946)	BVK820-829	Guy BTX	MCCW H60D	1935	1949	
40 (renumbered 340 1946)	CVK52	Karrier E6A	MCCW H60D	1935	1950	
41-43 (renumbered 341-43 1946)	DTN141-143	Karrier E6A	MCCW H60D	1936	1949-50	
44-46 (renumbered 344-46 1946)	DTN144-146	Guy BTX	MCCW H60D	1936	1949	
47-56 (renumbered 347-56 1946)	ETN47-56	Karrier E6A	MCCW H60D	1937	1949	

Fleet number	Registration	Chassis	Body	New	Withdrawn	Notes
57-66 (renumbered 357-66 1946)	ETN57-66	Guy BTX	MCCW H60D	1937	1948-49	
67-77 (renumbered 365-77 1946)	ETN67-77	AEC 664T	MCCW H60D	1937	1949-50	
78 (renumbered 378 1946)	FBB78	Guy BTX	Roe H60D	1937	1949	
79-84 (renumbered 379-84 1946)	FVK79-84	AEC 664T	Roe H60D	1938	1950	
85-98 (renumbered 385-98 1946)	FKV85-98	Karrier E6A	MCCW H60D	1938	1949	
99-108 (renumbered 399-408 1946)	FVK99-108	Guy BTX	MCCW H60D	1938	1949	
109 (renumbered 409 1946)	FVK109	Guy BTX	NCB H60D	1938	1949	
112 (renumbered 412 1946)	DHP112	Daimler CTM6	MCCW H60D	1938	1950	Numbers 110 and 111 not used
113-18 (renumbered 413-418 1946)	HVK113-118	Karrier E6A	Roe H60D	1939-40	1950	
119-24 (renumbered 419-24 1946)	HKV119-124	Karrier E6A	MCCW H60D	1940	1950	
1-9, 0 (1-5, 7 renumbered 301-5/07 1946)	KW9461/ 9463/ 9453-9455/ 6063/ 9460/6656/ 6655/ 9464	EE E11	EE H56R	1929-31	1943-1948	Ex-Bradford 592/94/84-86/ 73/91/80/79/95; acquired 1942; 0 acquired for spares only; 6, 8 and 9 did not enter service
125-42 (renumbered 425-42 1946)	JTN955-966/ JVK277-282	Karrier W	PR UH56R (Weymann UH56R on 137 and 138)	1944-45	1953-56	
443-78	LBB43-78	Sunbeam F4	MCCW H56R	1948-49	1961-63	8ft wide
479-98	LTN479-498	BUT 9641T	MCCW H70R	1948	1964-65	8ft wide
499-528	LTN499-528	Sunbeam S7	NCB H70R	1948-49	1963-65	501 preserved

Fleet number	Registration	Chassis	Body	New	Withdrawn	Notes
529-53	LTN529-553	Sunbeam F4	NCB H56R	1949-50	1963-64	
554-78	LTN554-578	BUT 9611T	NCB H56R	1949	1964	
579-628	NBB579-628	BUT 9641T	MCCW H70R	1950	1965-66	8ft wide; 628 preserved
Wartime loans						
11-15	FUF11-15	AEC 661T	Weymann H54R	1939	1942	Ex-Brighton 11-15; in service June 1942; returned October 1942
72, 73, 77-79, 82, 87, 123/45	AEL400-401/405-407/410, ALJ63, ALJ997, BEL830	Sunbeam MS2	PR or EE H56D	1934-35	1943-45	Ex-Bournemouth 72 etc; in service October 1942 to May 1945; 72, 73, 82, 87 and 145 returned to Bournemouth 1945; 77 transferred to Llanelly & District October 1943; 78, 79 & 123 transferred to South Shields March 1943

Route numbers in use from 1935-48	From	To	Operated from	Operated until	Notes
4/4A/4B/4C/4D	Denton Burn Loop, Denton Burn Boundary, Fox & Hounds	St Nicholas Cathedral, Walker, Wallsend Park Road	2 October 1935	30 October 1948	4 Fox & Hounds to Wallsend; 4A Fox & Hounds to Walker; 4B Denton Burn Loop or Boundary to St Nicholas; 4C St Nicholas to Fox & Hounds; 4D Wallsend or Walker to St Nicholas. 4B peak hour services extended from Denton Burn Boundary to Denton Square 24 April 1938. Denton Burn Loop abandoned 30 June 1941; thereafter 4B ran through to Denton Square, with short workings to Fox & Hounds

Route numbers in use from 1935-48	From	To	Operated from	Operated until	Notes
5A/5B/5C	Brighton Grove, Pilgrim Street	Walker (Church Street, Welbeck Road or Westbourne Avenue)	19 September 1939	30 October 1948	5A Brighton Grove to Church Street, 5B Brighton Grove to Welbeck Road, 5C Pilgrim Street to Westbourne Avenue. 5C extended from Pilgrim Street to Delaval Road 30 November 1947
5	Denton Square	Walker (to Church Street, from Welbeck Road)	24 April 1938	30 October 1948	Alternate services extended beyond Brighton Grove to Denton Square
6	Fenham (Two Ball Lonnen)	Central Station	1 August 1938	22 November 1941	Reverser initially in Ovington Grove
9	Osborne Road	Central Station	2 September 1938	29 November 1947	Service linked with number 3 group 30 November 1947 to run from Denton Road, etc, to Osborne Road. Number 9 was then no longer in use
12	Wallsend Boundary (Walkerville)	Central Station	2 September 1938	29 June 1941	Rerouted from Central Station to Denton Road to replace service 4B 30 June 1941
12	Wallsend Boundary (Walkerville)	Denton Road Terminus	30 June 1941	30 October 1948	Replaced by service 32 Wallsend Boundary to Fenham 1 November 1948
6	Fenham (Bingfield Gardens)	Central Station	23 November 1941	30 October 1948	Extended from Ovington Grove to reverser in Bingfield Gardens
3/3A/3B	Denton Road, Delaval Road, Benwell Church	Monument	11 June 1944	29 November 1947	3 from Denton Road, 3A from Delaval Road, 3B from Nichol Street (Benwell Church)
3/3A/3B	Denton Road, Delaval Road, Benwell Church	Monument, Osborne Road	30 November 1947	30 October 1948	Service linked with number 9 to form through services 3/3A to Osborne Road, 3B short workings to Monument
5C	Delaval Road, Benwell Church, Pilgrim Street	Walker (Westbourne Avenue)	30 November 1947	30 October 1948	Previous 5C extended from Pilgrim Street to Delaval Road

Route numbers in use from 1948-66	From	To	Operated from	Operated until	Notes
31/31A/31B	Central Station	Hollywood Avenue, Grange Estate, Polwarth Drive, Gosforth Par	18 April 1948	1 February 1964	31 to Gosforth Park, 31A to Polwarth Drive, 31B to Hollywood Avenue (Gosforth Stadium). 31A and 31B rerouted to Grange Estate from 28 October 1951. 31B re-routed to Polwarth Drive circa 1957. From 1951, Hollywood Avenue used only for 31B short workings and Gosforth Stadium services. Service 31B ran via Percy Street (Newgate Steet outbound, Clayton Street inbound)
32 (renumbered from 12)	Wallsend Boundary (Walkerville)	Fenham (Bingfield Gardens)	1 November 1948	29 May 1965	Rerouted from Denton Road Terminus to Fenham (Bingfield Gardens) and renumbered from 12 to 32
33/33A/33B (renumbered from 3/3A/3B)	Denton Road, Delaval Road, Benwell Church	Monument, Osborne Road	1 November 1948	29 May 1965	33 Denton Road to Osborne Road, 33A Delaval Road to Osborne Road, 33B short workings to Benwell Church or Monument. 33 merged with 43/44 route from 21 October 1956
34/34A/34B (renumbered from 4/4A/4B/4C/4D)	Denton Square, Fox & Hounds	St Nicholas Cathedral, Walker, Wallsend Park Road	1 November 1948	2 June 1963	34 F&H to Wallsend, 34A F&H to Walker, 34B F&H or Denton Square or Wallsend/Walker to St Nicholas. All but peak hour services extended from Fox & Hounds to Denton Square 1 August 1955
35/35A/35B (renumbered from 5/5A/5B)	Denton Square, Brighton Grove	Walker (Church Street or Welbeck Road)	1 November 1948	1 October 1966	35 Denton Square to Church Street, 35A Brighton Grove to Church Street, 35B Brighton Grove to Welbeck Road. Revised 35/35A to foot of Church Street via Welbeck Road, 35B to Westbourne Avenue 22 August 1965

Route numbers in use from 1948-66	From	To	Operated from	Operated until	Notes
35C (renumbered from 5C)	Delaval Road, Benwell Church, Pilgrim Street	Walker (Westbourne Avenue)	1 November 1948	1 October 1966	
36 (renumbered from 6)	Central Station	Fenham (Bingfield Gardens)	1 November 1948	29 May 1965	Renumbered from service 6 on 1 November 1948. Merged with 43/44 route 21 October 1956
38	Denton Road Terminus	Benton Road (Swarland Avenue) via Jesmond Road	1 November 1948	1 February 1964	Extended to Broadwood Road in 1962
39	Monument (Eldon Square)	Benton Park Road Circular (via Jesmond Road or North Road)	1 November 1948	15 January 1949	Number 39 initially used in both directions. Service extended to Central Station 16 January 1949
37	Denton Road Terminus	Benton Road (Swarland Avenue) via Heaton Road	16 January 1949	1 February 1964	Extended to Broadwood Road in 1962
39	Central Station	Benton Park Road Circular (via Jesmond Road and North Road)	16 January 1949	1 February 1964	Extended to Central Station 16 January 1949. Service 40 operated in reverse direction. Revised to run from/to Newgate Street 1 April 1962
40	Central Station	Benton Park Road Circular (via North Road and Jesmond Road)	16 January 1949	1 February 1964	Service 39 operated in reverse direction. Revised to run from/to Newgate Street 1 April 1962
41	Central Station	Heaton Road Circular (via Jesmond Road and Shields Road)	16 January 1949	29 May 1965	Service 42 operated in reverse direction. Revised to run from Newgate Street to Central Station 1 April 1962
42	Central Station	Heaton Road Circular (via Shields Road and Jesmond Road)	16 January 1949	29 May 1965	Service 41 operated in reverse direction. Revised to run from Central Station to Newgate Street 1 April 1962

Route numbers in use from 1948-66	From	To	Operated from	Operated until	Notes
43/44 (incorporating 33 and 36)	Central Station	Osborne Road (via Fenham)	21 October 1956	29 May 1965	43 Osborne Road to Denton Road; 36 Denton Road to Central Station; 44 Central Station to Fenham; 33 Fenham to Osborne Road

Pictured awaiting departure from in front of Clarendon Hotel on Berwick Street with a service on route 42 is Sunbeam F4 No 550. This was one of twenty-five 7ft 6in wide vehicles that represented the last Sunbeams acquired by the corporation entering service between December 1949 and March 1950. No 550 was one of the batch that survived in service until early February 1964, being scrapped four months later. *J. Joyce/Online Transport Archive*

OLDHAM

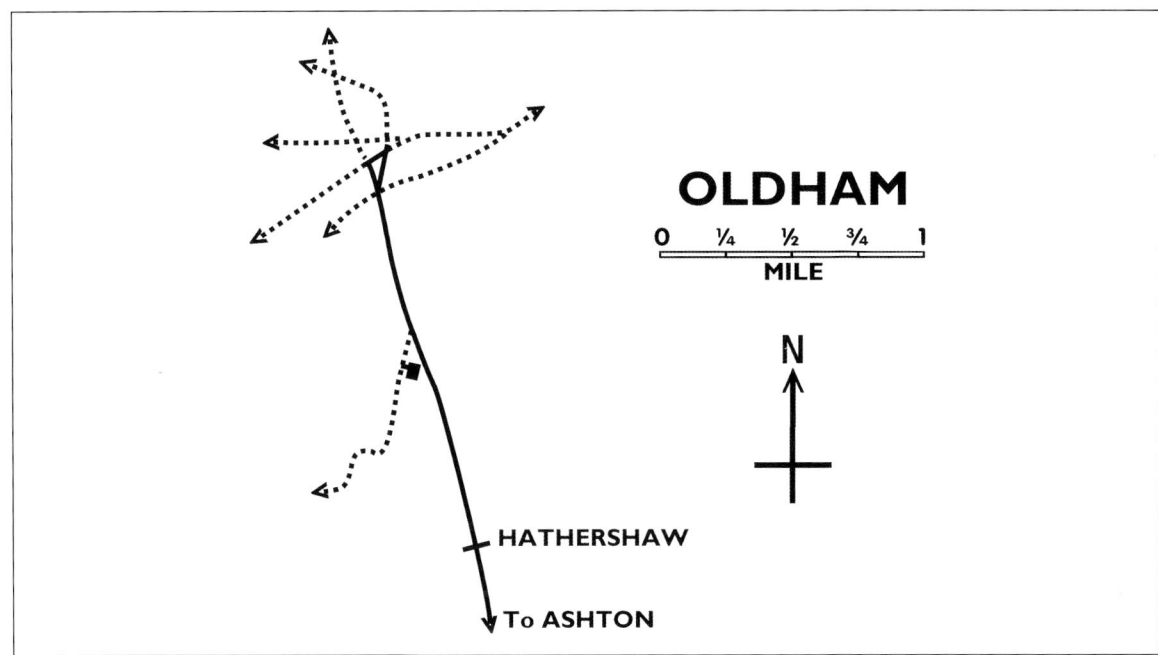

From 1921, when Ashton Corporation acquired those sections of the Oldham, Ashton & Hyde Tramways Co (a subsidiary of BET) within its boundaries, a through standard gauge tramway service operated between the two towns. Despite its name, the company never actually reached Oldham itself, only the boundary at Hathershaw with the section from Hathershaw to Oldham itself being acquired earlier by the corporation from the Manchester, Bury, Rochdale & Oldham Steam Tramway Co and electrified.

In 1923, Ashton Corporation proposed that, due to the state of the track on its section of the route (the cost of replacement as double track was considered prohibitive at £77,000 whilst the cheaper option of a single track with passing loops was still estimated to cost £38,000), trolleybuses be introduced and parliamentary powers for their introduction were obtained. The cost of installing the trolleybus overhead and the purchase of vehicles was estimated to be £26,000.

To operate the new trolleybus service, ten vehicles were acquired, eight being owned by Ashton and two by Oldham; the latter were housed in the corporation's Copsterhill Road depot. With work completed, the new through service was introduced on 26 August 1925. Although Ashton ceased the operation of its tram route at the same time, Oldham continued to operate trams in parallel to the trolleybus service and, as both forms of transport shared the same overhead, this caused problems and often delayed services, A further problem was the noise generated by the solid-tyred vehicles, which caused annoyance to the local residents.

In June 1923, Edward May Munro (who had joined the RET Construction Co Ltd as chief engineer before the First World War) left the company. By this date, the company had been re-established as Railless Ltd, a subsidiary of Short Bros (Rochester and Bedford) Ltd, and after Munro's departure the business was further reorganised. In 1924, a new model, with a lower floor – at 2ft 4in – than achieved previously was launched. The first customers for the new model were Ashton and Oldham corporations with the order for ten being split eight and two respectively. The duo acquired by Oldham became Nos 1 and 2 but were destined for a very short operational life as Oldham decided to cease trolleybus operation. Last operated on 5 September 1926, the pair were stored for some four years before being sold to Ashton where they were cannibalised for spare parts. *Railless/Geoff Lumb Collection*

The new route, which extended over some four route miles, was equipped with a turning loops in both Ashton and Oldham town centres with short workings at Waterloo and Hathershaw, on the Ashton section, that were equipped with a reversing triangle and a loop respectively.

The problems faced by Oldham allied to the fact that the track on its section was in much better condition led the corporation to decide to cease trolleybus operation. The last Oldham trolleybuses operated on 5 September 1926 with trams continuing to provide a service to the boundary. Ashton, however, continued to operate trolleybuses on its section, thus severing the through service between the two towns.

Fleet number	Registration	Chassis	Body	New	Withdrawn	Notes
1 and 2	BY3861/3854	Railless LFT30 (actually constructed by Short Bros of Rochester)	Short B36C	1925	1926	The remains of the two were sold to Ashton Corporation in two deals during 1930 as sources of spares

Route number	From	To	Date Opened	Date Closed	Notes
N/A	Town Centre	Hathershaw	26 August 1925	5 September 1926	Joint service with Ashton-under-Lyne

RAMSBOTTOM

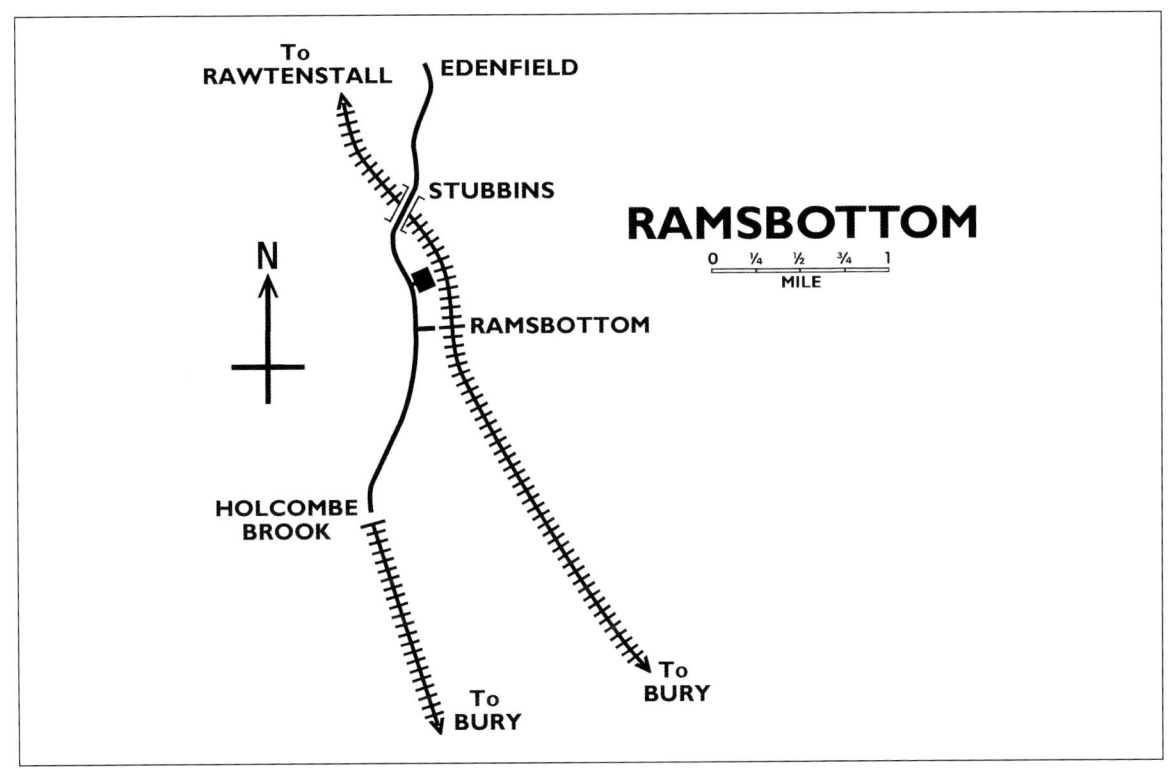

Unusually amongst British trolleybus operators, Ramsbottom UDC had no experience as a tramway operator although it had gained powers – under an Act of 1903 – to introduce trams to the district.

Having failed to introduce trams, the UDC decided at a meeting on 11 January 1912 to seek powers to operate trolleybuses; these were obtained following the passage of the Ramsbottom Urban District Railless Traction Act of 1912. These powers also extended to the possible conversion of the system to tram operation if desired.

The initial route authorised provided a connection from the Lancashire & Yorkshire Railway branch terminus at Holcombe Brook through Ramsbottom itself to terminate at Edenfield. In addition to the main route, there was also a short branch from Ramsbottom town centre to serve the town's railway station (on the Lancashire & Yorkshire Railway's Bury to Rawtenstall line – today's preserved East Lancashire Railway). The newly-acquired trolleybuses were housed in a new depot constructed between Ramsbottom and Stubbins at Stubbins Lane.

Initially four vehicles were acquired from the Railless Electric Traction Co Ltd; these were ordered in early 1913 and the first was delivered on 10 August 1913, four days before the official – and successful – Board of Trade inspection. Public services were

Pictured in front of the Hare & Hounds public house, which is still extant, at the southern terminus of Ramsbottom's trolleybus route is one of the quartet – No 2 – of the single-deck vehicles supplied by RET with Milnes Voss twenty-eight-seat bodywork. The solid tyres allied to the granite setts played havoc with the bodywork on these four vehicles with the result that all were rebuilt by Lockwood & Clarkson during the war. At this time, Nos 2 and 3 switched numbers. All four received replacement chassis – probably supplied by Thornycroft – during 1923 and 1924 and were also rebodied at the same time by Short Bros. *D.W.K. Jones Collection/Online Transport Archive*

introduced using the one available vehicle at 6pm that same day – Thursday 14 August. The remaining three vehicles were all delivered by the end of the following week.

Granite setts and solid tyres were not a recipe for long life for the trolleybus bodies and, in order to facilitate their rebuilding, a further two vehicles were purchased in 1915; the original four vehicles were rebuilt between 1915 and 1917. These six vehicles sufficed until 1922 when a seventh was purchased; this was constructed by Short Bros of Rochester and was demonstrated at Dover prior to delivery.

In 1923, the UDC introduced a bus service from Edenfield to Rawtenstall; this was taken over by Rawtenstall Corporation on 1 September the following year. Two months later – on 21 November 1924 – a through service, operated by Bury, Ramsbottom and Rawtenstall was launched linking the three towns; thereafter the trolleybuses were on borrowed time.

In 1926, courtesy of the Ramsbottom UDC Act, the council obtained greater powers to operate motorbuses and gradually the trolleybus service was reduced. Although the last services operated – without ceremony – on 31 December 1930 (although, officially, services continued 31 March 1931) – trolleybus operation had been much curtailed since 1928 with only one vehicle licensed after March 1930.

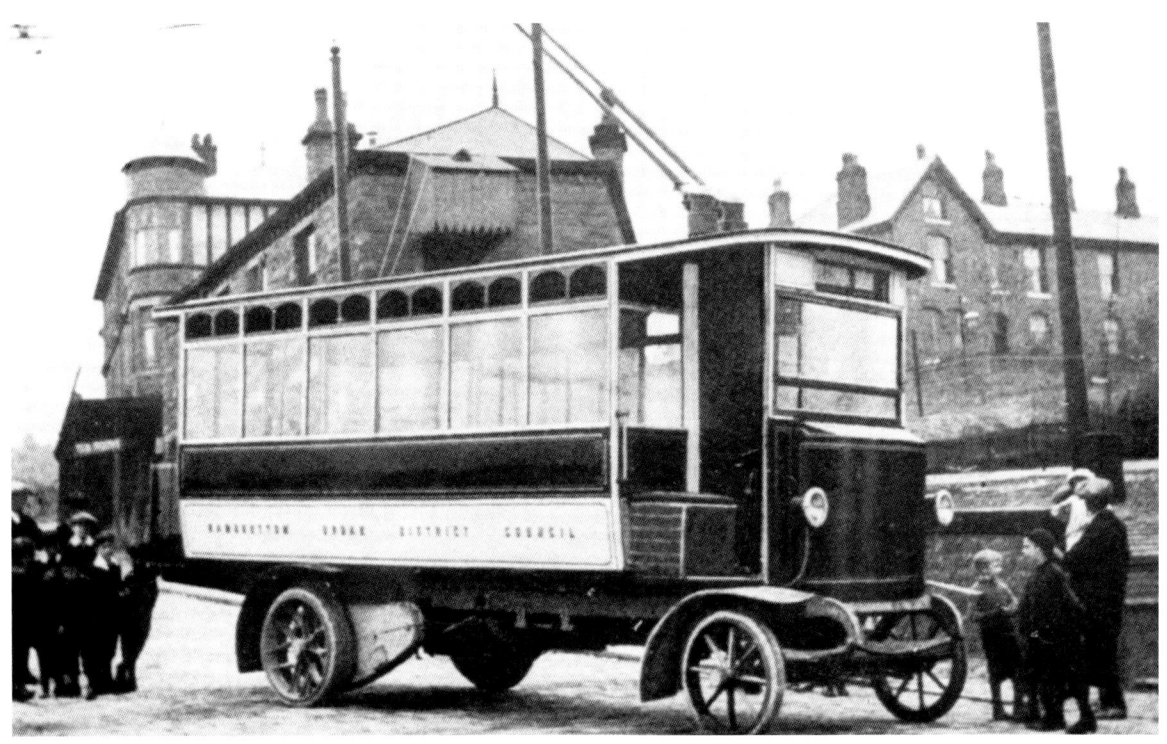

The offside of one of the initial quartet of RET-supplied trolleybuses pictured at Edenfield when new. *D.W.K. Jones Collection/Online Transport Archive*

In all, Ramsbottom operated seven trolleybuses during the eighteen years that the main route operated; although impossible to identify a fleet number, the style of bodywork would suggest that this is one of the original quartet as rebuilt by Short Bros during 1923 and 1924. In 1926, powers were obtained to operate buses and the launch of a through bus service from Bury to Rawtenstall in November that year resulted in buses duplicating the section operated by trolleybus. The trolleybus operation was reduced to part day only in October 1929 with only two vehicles licensed; this was reduced to one in March the following year. This final trolleybus survived until the system's abandonment on 31 December 1930. *D.W.K. Jones Collection/Online Transport Archive*

Fleet number	Registration	Chassis	Body	New	Withdrawn	Notes
1-4 (2 and 3 swopped identities in about 1916)	TB8570-8572 allocated in 1921 to three of the fleet	RET (built by David Brown; received replacement chassis in 1923-24 [possibly supplied by Thornycroft])	Milnes Voss B28R (rebodied by Lockwood & Clarkson 1915-17; further rebuilt by Short Bros 1923-24)	1913	By 1931	
5	TB8573 from 1921	RET	Lockwood & Clarkson B26R	1915	1927	
6	TD417 from 1925 (out of service when registrations first introduced and registered only in 1925 when reinstated)	RET (new chassis 1924 supplied [possibly by Thornycroft])	Lockwood & Clarkson B26R (rebuilt by Roe 1924)	1915	1928	
7	TD418 from 1925 (original registration unknown and reregistered in 1925 when reinstated)	Railless Ltd (built by Short Bros of Rochester)	Short Bros B26R	1922	1928	

Route number	From	To	Date Opened	Date Closed	Notes
N/A	Holcombe Brook	Edenfield	14 August 1913	31 December 1930 (officially 31 March 1931)	
N/A	Market Place	Railway station	14 August 1913	31 December 1930 (officially 31 March 1931)	

ST HELENS

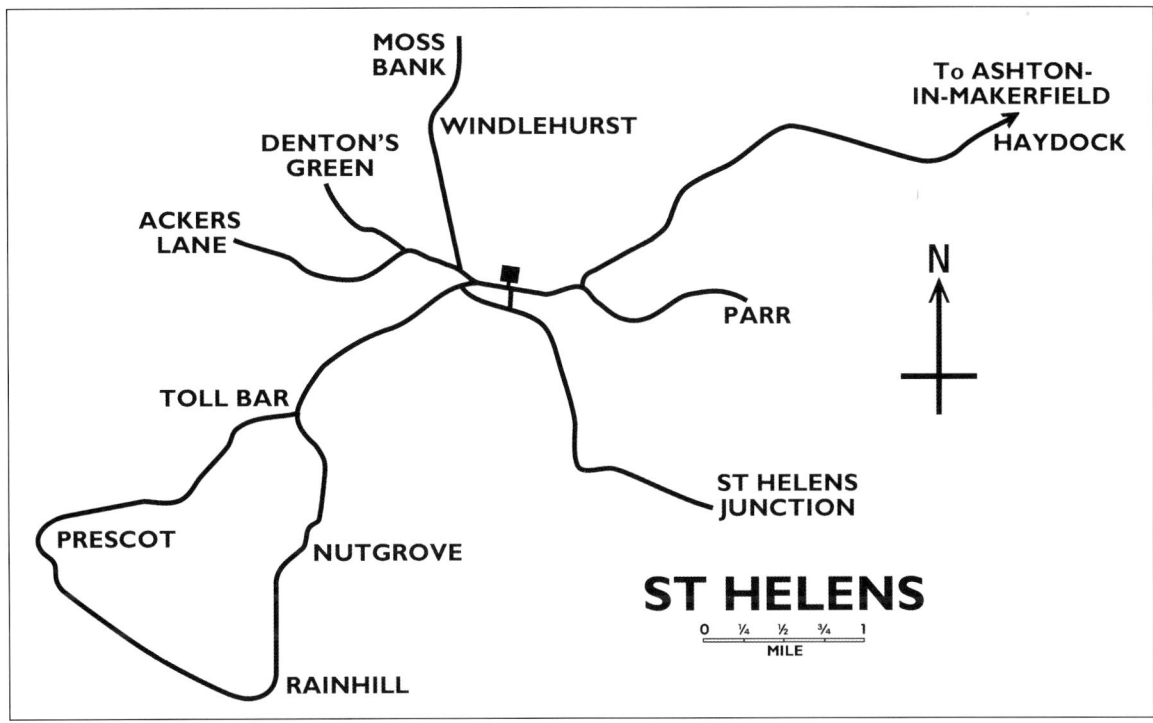

St Helens Corporation was a relatively late entrant to the list of municipal transport operators. A horse tramway had existed in the town from 1881 and, in 1889, this was acquired by the St Helens & District Tramway Co Ltd and most routes saw steam traction replace horses. Although the corporation had acquired the track, following an Act of 1893, it leased the operation to the company for 21 years from 1 October 1898. A second company – appropriately called the New St Helens & District Tramways Co Ltd – was created to raise the capital to electrify the system and a replacement lease to the new company was issued on 1 February 1899. Work started on electrification, and the first electric trams commenced operation on 7 April 1900. The network eventually expanded to almost nineteen route miles offering direct connections with the tramways operated by Liverpool Corporation and the South Lancashire Tramways.

The company lease expired on 30 September 1919 and, the following day, the corporation assumed operation of the network. It inherited a fleet of thirty-six trams with an additional number of SLT trams loaned to make up for a shortage of vehicles. The corporation was an enthusiastic new owner, undertaking track replacement and purchasing a batch of eight new double-deck trams from Brush in 1921 with some of the older cars rebuilt. On 1 August 1921, the corporation introduced its first motorbuses but the tramway was to dominate until the second half of the decade; powers to operate both

Right: **In 1934** and 1935 St Helens took delivery of two batches of Leyland TBD2s; the first five – Nos 121-25 – were fitted with Brush fifty-six-seat bodywork whilst the remaining eleven – Nos 126-36 – had bodywork supplied by Massey. All were rebodied by East Lancs between 1945 and 1947 and it is in this condition that No 125 is pictured at the Ackers Lane terminus of route 5. This route was one of a number of services converted to bus operation in early February 1952; all sixteen of the Leyland TBD2s were withdrawn that year. *Harry Luff/Online Transport Archive*

Below: **Having previously** acquired a number of vehicles from Ransomes, Sims & Jefferies earlier in the decade, St Helens returned to that supplier during 1936 and 1937 for a batch of eight D4s – Nos 137-44 – equipped with Massey fifty-seat bodywork as evinced by No 138 pictured here on a route 3A service to Blackbrook; this was a short working of the route to Haydock and terminated at the borough boundary. All of the batch were withdrawn between 1949 and 1952. *Geoffrey Ashwell/Online Transport Archive*

St Helens acquired two batches of Leyland TBD2s fitted with Massey fifty-seat bodywork; Nos 126-36 were new in 1935 whilst Nos 101-04 arrived two years later. The earlier batch was rebodied by East Lancs between 1944 and 1948 whilst the latter were rebodied by the same company during 1947 and 1948. Here one of the later batch – No 102 in rebodied form – is seen on a route 3A service to Blackbrook; this was a short working for the longer service to Haydock. Although No 126-36 were withdrawn during 1952 Nos 101-04 survived to be renumbered 301-04 during 1955 before being withdrawn the following year. *Peter Grace/John Laker Collection*

motorbuses and trolleybuses were granted in the St Helens Corporation Act 1921, which received the Royal Assent on 4 August 1921.

That St Helens was interested in the possible operation of trolleybuses is indicated by the fact that, on 7 August 1924, the Royal Assent was given to the St Helens Corporation (Trolley Vehicles) Order Confirmation Act 1924. Nothing, however, progressed at this stage but, on 29 July 1927, a further piece of legislation – the St Helens Corporation (Trolley Vehicles) Order Confirmation Act 1927 – received the Royal Assent.

The rationale for the renewed powers lay in the desire to test the operation of trolleybuses on a 2¾-mile section of the existing tramway – the predominantly single track section from the mental hospital at Nutgrove to Prescot – where the track was life expired and the cost of replacement could not be justified. Due to its condition, the route had been operated by motorbus since 1923.

For the launch of the new service on 11 July 1927, four single-deck trolleybuses were supplied by Garrett. The fleet was accommodated in the corporation's depot on Hall Street, access being gained through the use of a skate with the existing tram track and overhead. The next service to be converted to trolleybus operation was that to Parr, which again had been operated by motorbus since the trams were withdrawn in 1928. Services on this section – which extended half-a-mile beyond the original tram terminus – were introduced on 30 July 1929 and resulted, for the first time, in trolleybus overhead in the town centre. Six further single-deckers, supplied by Ransomes, Sims & Jefferies, were delivered during 1928 and 1929 for this new service.

The first double-deckers were delivered in 1931; these were the only three-axle trolleybuses owned by St Helens and their arrival coincided with the conversion of the route to Haydock on 21 June 1931. This provided a direct connection with the trolleybuses operated by the South Lancashire Transport Co and facilitated the introduction of a joint through service linking St Helens with Atherton.

Although there was now a three-year gap before the next conversion, the period thereafter, between 1934 and 1936, saw the considerable expansion of the trolleybus network and the final elimination of the corporation's tramway network. The first of these new routes was that to Moss Bank via Windle – which had been bus operated since the trams were withdrawn in 1932 – which commenced operation on 16 May 1934. This was followed on 4 July 1934 by the introduction of trolleybuses to the route from the town centre to the mental hospital at Nutgrove on 4 July 1934; this meant that, for the first time, the trolleybuses used on the original section were able to access the depot without use of the skate. St Helens Corporation (Trolley Vehicles) Order Confirmation Act 1934 which received the Royal Assent on 12 July 1934 authorised the conversion of a further eight miles of tramway. Two routes were converted during 1935; these were to St Helens Junction on 1 May and to Denton's Green on 29 May. This left only one section of tramway operational – the key route from the town centre to Prescot – which was last operated by tram on 31 March 1936 with the replacement trolleybuses taking over the next day.

On 16 May 1950 No 146 is pictured in St Helens; this was one of a batch of twelve Massey-bodied Ransomes, Sims & Jefferies trolleybuses – Nos 145-56 – that were delivered in 1938. These were the last new trolleybuses acquired before the Second World War and were largely acquired to replace the early single-deckers delivered between 1927 and 1929 which were withdrawn between 1936 and 1940. Unlike some a number of earlier purchases, Nos 135-56 were not rebodied after the Second World War and were thus relatively early casualties, all being withdrawn between 1950 and 1952. *C. Carter/Online Transport Archive*

St Helens was one of a number of operators that received new trolleybuses during the Second World War that had originally been ordered by operators in South Africa, but which were diverted to the domestic market. In the case of St Helens, ten Sunbeam MF2s with Massey fifty-seat bodywork were delivered during 1942. Nos 157-66 had originally been ordered by Johannesburg and represented the first 8ft 0in-wide trolleybuses to be operated by the corporation. No 162 – one of the eight to be reseated in 1951 – is also pictured in St Helens on 16 May 1950 outside the market on Bridge Street with an outbound service on route 8. The ten were renumbered 357-66 in 1955 but all had been withdrawn by the end of the following year. *C. Carter/Online Transport Archive*

The trolleybuses proved a success with the operating margins significantly better than the motorbus fleet whilst the use of cross-town routes meant that the wiring in town centre was simpler than it might have been. In 1938, it was noted in *Transport World* that 'the policy governing development of facilities is that trolleybuses will be intensified in frequency of service as required on existing routes, whereas buses will be used to develop new districts in outlying areas.' This did not preclude the expansion of the trolleybus network – indeed the St Helens Corporation (Trolley Vehicles) Order Confirmation Act 1939, which received the Royal Assent on 13 July 1939, authorised the construction of five miles of new route – but these developments were not progressed and it was not until 29 June 1943 – when the Ackers Lane branch off the Green Lane route opened – that the system was further extended. This was, however, destined to be the last extension.

During the war and immediately after it, the corporation received twenty Sunbeam double-deckers including ten which had been originally ordered by Johannesburg but which had been diverted to St Helens as a result of the war. In 1951, a further sixteen new trolleybuses were received; these were the first highbridge-bodied double-deckers in the fleet and had to be fitted with a special device to ensure that they did not try to pass under the low railway bridge at Pleasley Cross on the St Helens Junction route.

However, the new arrivals came after the abrupt decision made the same year to convert the system to bus operation had been made. The first conversions – on 2 February 1952 – saw buses replace trolleybuses on the routes to Moss Bank, St Helens Junction and Denton's Green. These conversions were followed on 12 November 1955 when the all-day service on the route to Parr ceased; it continued to see a peak hour trolleybus service until 9 November 1956. On 11 November 1956, the through trolleybus to Atherton was withdrawn. This left trolleybuses operating only the Prescot loop and this was to survive for a further eighteen months. Public trolleybus services over the route ceased on 30 June 1958; the following day saw the official last trolleybus when No 374 carried the official party on a farewell trip.

After the closure, the two post-war batches of trolleybuses were sold; half went to South Shields Corporation with the other eight being acquired by Bradford Corporation. As Nos 794-801, the eight remained in service in the West Riding until withdrawn between November 1965 and June 1971; one of the last two to survive – Bradford No 799 (ex-St Helens No 387) – was secured for preservation in late 1971 and has subsequently been restored to its St Helens livery.

In 1945, St Helens Corporation took delivery of a batch of ten Sunbeam Ws – Nos 105-14 – which were fitted with Roe-built lowbridge fifty-seat bodywork. The route between St Helens and Atherton, which was jointly operated with SLT, required the use of lowbridge vehicles as a result of restricted height bridges. During the summer of 1953, one of the batch is seen in Atherton. The ten were renumbered 305-14 in 1955 and were withdrawn between 1956 and 1958; No 305 was amongst those taken out of service in 1956. The St Helens to Atherton service was converted to bus operation on 11 November 1956. *Phil Tatt/Online Transport Archive*

Pictured in front of the Prescot Reform Club on Warrington Road is St Helens No 176. This was one of eight Sunbeam F4s – Nos 174-81 – fitted with fifty-five-seat bodywork supplied by East Lancs and entered service in December 1950 or January 1951. These were the first highbridge trolleybuses to be operated by St Helens and were used primarily on the Prescot service. They had a relatively short wheelbase to facilitate operation over the hump-back bridge on Thato Heath Road. Renumbered 374-81 in 1955, all eight remained in service until the final conversion on 30 June 1958 with No 374 acting as the official last trolleybus the following day. The eight were sold, after withdrawal, to South Shields. Behind No 176 can be seen the overhead heading to the north that formed the short-working loop in Prescot. *Marcus Eavis/Online Transport Archive*

In 1955, all of the St Helens surviving trolleybuses were renumbered, with 200 being added to their original fleet number; as a result, the final batch of trolleybuses purchased – eight BUT 9611TS fitted with East Lancs fifty-six-bodywork – which had been Nos 182-89 became Nos 382-89 and it is post-renumbering that No 383 is pictured at Prescot. Following the conversion of the circular route via Prescot and Rainhill on 30 June 1958, the eight BUTs were sold to Bradford where they became Nos 794-801. Withdrawn eventually during 1971, No 387 (ex-Bradford No 799) was preserved. *Harry Luff/Online Transport Archive*

Fleet number	Registration	Chassis	Body	New	Withdrawn	Notes
1-4 (renumbered 101-04 in 1929 and 101/03/04 renumbered 161/63/64 in 1937)	DJ3243-3246	Garrett	RS&J B35C	1927	1936-38	
5 (renumbered 100 in 1929 and 110 in 1934)	DJ3684	RS&J	RS&J B32C	1928	1938	
105-09	DJ4081-4084/ ET5968	RS&J	RS&JB35C	1929	1938-40	109 loaned to and registered by Rotherham 1929
110-14 (110 renumbered 115 in 1934)	DJ4845-4849	RS&J	RS&J L60R	1931	1942	
116-120	DJ6051-6055	RS&J D4	Brush L50R (119 rebodied by East Lancs [L50R] in 1943)	1934	1945-50	
121-25	DJ6106/6120-6123	Leyland TBD2	Brush L50R (rebodied by East Lancs [L50R] 1945-47)	1934	1952	
126-36	DJ6453-6463	Leyland TBD2	Massey L50R (rebodied by East Lancs [L50R] 1944-48)	1935	1952	
137-44	DJ6863-6867/7236-7238	RS&J D4	Massey L50R	1936	1949-52	
101-04 (renumbered 301-04 in 1955)	DJ7428-7431	Leyland TBD2	Massey L50R (rebodied by East Lancs [L50R] 1947-48)	1937	1956	
145-56	DJ8120-8131	RS&J D4	Massey L50R	1938	1950-52	
157-66 (renumbered 357-66 in 1955)	DJ9005-9014	Sunbeam MF2	Massey L50R (all bar 161 and 163 reseated to L56R in 1951)	1942	1955-56	Diverted from an order originally destined for Johannesburg in South Africa; were the first 8ft 0in wide trolleybuses in the fleet

Fleet number	Registration	Chassis	Body	New	Withdrawn	Notes
105-14 (renumbered 305-14 in 1955)	DJ9183-9192	Sunbeam W	Roe UL50R	1945	1956-58	
174-181 (renumbered 374-81 in 1955)	BDJ74-81	Sunbeam F4	East Lancs H55R	1950-51	1958	Sold to South Shields
182-89 (renumbered 382-89 in 1955)	BDJ82-89	BUT 9611T	East Lancs H56R	1951	1958	Sold to Bradford; 387 preserved

Route number	From	To	Date Opened	Date Closed	Notes
7/8	Nutgrove (Rainhill Mental Hospital)	Prescot	11 July 1927	30 June 1958	Eventually operated as a circle route 7 clockwork and 8 anti-clockwork; 9 was either a service to Prescot or a Toll Bar short working, 10 a short working to Nutgrove and 11 a short working to Portico
4	Town Centre	Parr	30 July 1929	9 November 1956	Peak hours only after 12 November 1955
1	Town Centre	Haydock	21 June 1931	11 November 1956	Link to SLT network with through services operated; route 3 was Haydock service with 3A being used for short workings to Huntsman Inn and Blackbrook
4	Town Centre	Moss Bank	16 May 1934	2 February 1952	
7/8	Town Centre	Nutgrove	4 July 1934	30 June 1958	Eventually operated as a circle route 7 clockwork and 8 anti-clockwork; 9 was either a service to Prescot or a Toll Bar short working, 10 a short working to Nutgrove and 11 a short working to Portico
6	Town Centre	St Helens Junction	1 May 1935	2 February 1952	
6	Town Centre	Denton's Green	29 May 1935	2 February 1952	
7/8	Toll Bar	Prescot	1 April 1936	30 June 1958	Eventually operated as a circle route 7 clockwork and 8 anti-clockwork; 9 was either a service to Prescot or a Toll Bar short working, 10 a short working to Nutgrove and 11 a short working to Portico
5	Green Lane	Ackers Lane	29 June 1943	2 February 1952	

SOUTH LANCASHIRE TRANSPORT

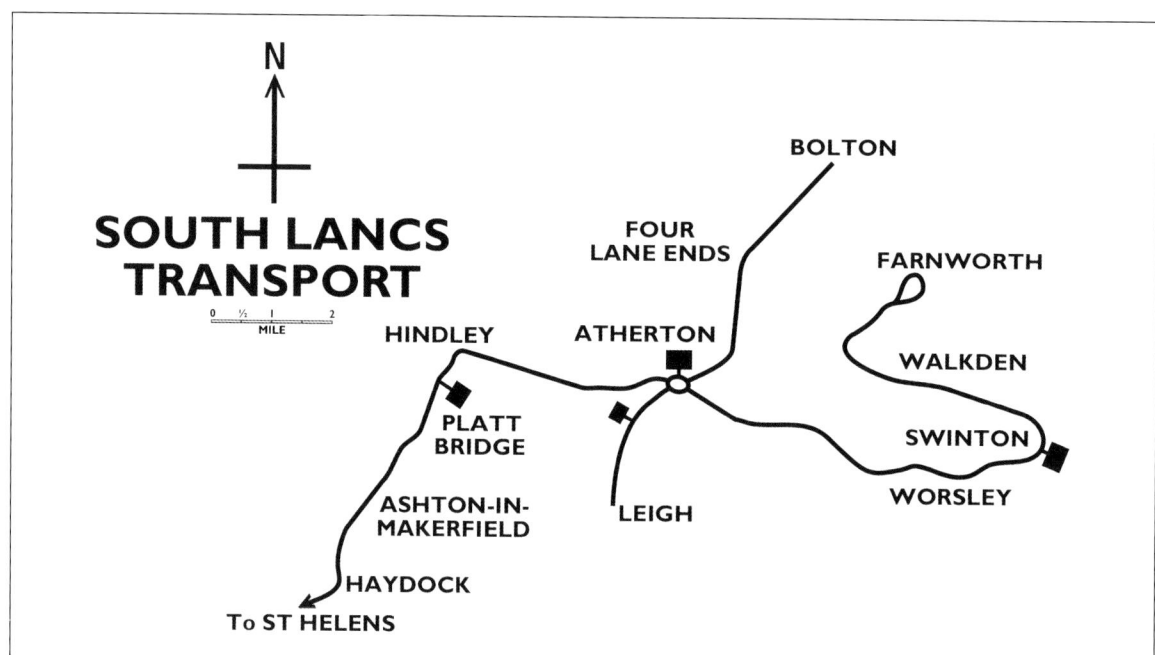

Centred on Atherton, the South Lancashire Tramways Co – a subsidiary initially of the South Lancashire Electric Traction & Power Co Ltd – operated a network of almost forty route miles at its peak. Apart from its own track, it also operated over lines leased from a number of small local authorities – such as Farnworth UDC and Hindley UDC – but early in its history both it and the South Lancashire Electric Traction & Power Co Ltd were forced into receivership in July 1904. The South Lancashire Tramways Co was saved eventually on 2 January 1906 becoming a subsidiary thereafter of Lancashire United Tramways Ltd. Although connections were made with a number of other tramways, through services initially only operated to Bolton but, in later years, joint agreements were made with the corporations of Manchester and Salford as well as with the New St Helens & District Tramways Co Ltd.

As for other tramway operators, the years after the First World War proved difficult for the company. Its fleet of trams – almost ninety in total – dated largely to the first decade of the twentieth century – although two new trams were obtained in 1927 – and so were increasingly outdated; moreover there were issues with the track. Lack of maintenance during the war was one problem, leading to a need for relaying, whilst the period had also witnessed a considerable growth in traffic which was proving difficult to handle on the largely single track sections. Lancashire United Tramways Ltd, which had launched its first motorbus service on 18 June 1920, was actively developing a network of bus routes. The future of the tramway looked grim.

For the opening of the route to Ashton-in-Makerfield on 3 August, South Lancashire Transport took delivery of ten Guy BTXs fitted with Roe sixty-seat bodywork. Seen in Atherton in original condition in about 1950, No 1 was one of two extensively rebuilt in 1953. Of the ten, Nos 5, 6, 8 and 10 had their front ends rebuilt between 1950 and 1955. Withdrawals of the batch commenced in 1956 with Nos 2, 3, 5, 8 and 9 being taken out of service; the remaining five succumbed in 1958. *Harry Luff/Online Transport Archive*

A clue as to the decision to adopt trolleybuses can perhaps be gleaned from part of the original holding company's name: '& Power Co Ltd'. Just as there was an incentive for municipal operators to opt for trolleybuses to replace trams to maintain business for the equally municipally-owned power stations, the loss of the power supplied to the tramway, should it be replaced by motorbus services, was not an attractive business proposition.

Under the terms of the South Lancashire Transport Act, 1929, which received the Royal Assent on 10 May 1929, the company was authorised to change its name to South Lancashire Transport – Lancashire United Tramways Ltd had already, in 1926, changed its name to the Lancashire United Tramways & Power Co Ltd – and to convert its tramway routes to trolleybus operation.

The first route to be converted to trolleybus was that from Atherton to Ashton-in-Makerfield; the last trams operated on 2 August 1930 with the trolleybuses taking over the next day. For the new service, Guy supplied ten double-deckers fitted with Roe

SLT No 1 is pictured again, this time in 1956 (after its 1953 rebuilding) when it was used on an Omnibus Society tour. Only one other vehicle from the batch – No 7 – underwent a similarly extensive rebuilding in 1953; both survived until 1958. *R.L. Wilson/Online Transport Archive*

bodywork; by the end of 1933, a total of forty-six trolleybuses had been delivered. The new trolleybuses were initially to be based at the erstwhile tram depot at Capps Street, Platt Bridge.

The original service was extended to Haydock on 21 June 1931; at Haydock, a connection was made to the St Helens system – which had opened to Haydock from the town centre on the same day – thus permitting the introduction of a new through service from Atherton to St Helens. This was followed on 19 August 1931 by the fourteen-mile circuitous route from Atherton to Farnworth. This resulted in the allocation of trolleybuses for the first time to another ex-tram depot, this time on Partington Road, Swinton. The same day also saw trolleybuses make use of the company's main depot – Leigh Road, Atherton – but until the conversion of the route to Leigh two years later, trolleybuses could only gain access to it using a skate allied to the tram track and overhead. These two were destined to be the company's last trolleybus depots at the cessation of services in August 1958.

Further trolleybus powers were confirmed in the South Lancashire Transport Company (Trolley Vehicles) Provisional Order Act 1932 that received the Royal Assent on 12 July 1932. The final company trams operated on 16 December 1933 on the route from Leigh to Bolton with trolleybuses taking over the following day. Motorbuses replaced trams on the section of the route beyond Leigh to Lowton St Mary's. This was not quite the end

For the opening of the Haydock and Farnworth sections in 1931, SLT purchased a further twenty Guy BTXs – Nos 11-30 – which were again fitted with Roe sixty-seat bodywork; the seating capacity of was reduced to fifty-six by 1932. Typical of the batch as delivered externally is No 15, which was recorded at the Atherton terminus during the summer of 1953. Of the twenty, fourteen had their front ends rebuilt between 1950 and 1955. Most of the six unrebuilt examples – including No 15 – were withdrawn during 1955 and 1956. *Phil Tatt/Online Transport Archive*

of company involvement with trams, however, as two sections of track – in Farnworth and from Winton to Worsley – were leased by the company but operated by Bolton and Salford corporations respectively; tram operation ceased on the Salford section on 7 October 1936 and in Farnworth on 12 November 1944. In both cases, corporation-owned motorbuses took over.

For the section of the Bolton from the borough boundary at Four Lane Ends to the town centre, the trolleybuses operated services alongside the trams of Bolton Corporation; this was to continue until 28 March 1936 when the tram service was withdrawn with trolleybuses taking over the following day. A further twelve trolleybuses – this time double-deckers supplied by Leyland – were delivered; although all were maintained and housed by the company, the legal ownership of the first four – Nos 48-51 – belonged to Bolton Corporation as its contribution for the Bolton local service to Four Lane Ends. The Guy trolleybuses were all lowbridge – to cater for a number of low railway bridges – the Leylands were highbridge and so were restricted to the Leigh to Bolton route.

The conversion of the Leigh to Bolton route effectively marked the end of the system's expansion although 1936 also saw the creation of the terminal loop in Farnworth via

No 28 was one of the 1931 batch of Guy BTXs with rebuilt front ends; it is pictured here in Atherton. Of the fourteen rebuilt examples, Nos 14, 17, 22, 25 and 30 were withdrawn during 1955 and 1956 whilst the remaining nine soldiered on until 1958. *Harry Luff/Online Transport Archive*

Market Street, Brackley Street and Albert Road. Apart from the diversion of the Bolton terminus in July 1948 into the new bus station on Howell Croft South, the Farnworth loop was the last significant change to the overhead.

During the war, the company's fleet was strengthened through the acquisition of six Utility-bodied Karrier Ws during 1943 and 1944. After the war, with Bolton having ceased to operate the section of company track in Farnworth – the section from Moses Gate to either Farnworth or Walkden – the company sought powers to convert them to trolleybus operation. These were granted by the South Lancashire Transport Act 1948, which received the Royal Assent on 30 June 1948. However, these plans were not progressed with although a further six new trolleybuses were acquired in 1948; Nos 66-71 proved to be the last new trolleybuses acquired by the company. During the period between 1950 and 1953, a number of the pre-war Guys underwent varying degrees of modernisation or rebuilding, which resulted in them displaying a much more modern image.

In 1955, E.H. Edwards, the company's managing director, retired at the age of 81; he had been employed by the company since 1911 and had overseen the conversion of the company's tramways to trolleybus operation and had been the system's greatest proponent since it had opened. It was, perhaps, no coincidence that the decision to replace the trolleybuses with motorbuses was taken less than six months after his retirement.

The first conversion occurred on 25 March 1956 when the Bolton local services were replaced; although the through service continued thereafter – although initially it had been thought that the Bolton to Leigh service was to have been the first to be abandoned this plan had been complicated by the desire of Leigh Corporation to be involved in any replacement motorbus service – the loop at Hulton Lane, used by the local services, was taken out of use. The four Bolton-owned trolleybuses were transferred to the corporation's Bridgeman Street depot – the first time they had been based at a corporation depot in their life – prior to disposal for scrap.

The next conversion saw the replacement of trolleybuses on the route to Haydock on 11 November 1956. This left two services outstanding – that to Farnworth and the Bolton to Leigh route – which were both to survive until 31 August 1958 although towards the end many of the trolleybus duties were actually being fulfilled by motorbus. The last trolleybus to operate was No 28, which ran from Farnworth to Swinton depot at 11.15pm reaching its destination at 11.50pm. All the Swinton-based trolleybuses – again with No 28 being the last – were then transferred to Leigh Road depot for disposal during the early hours of 1 September; they made this final trip on trade plates as the licences had already been surrendered for a refund.

Pictured when new, No 41 was one of sixteen Guy BTs – Nos 31-46 – purchased in 1933 for the opening of the route from Bolton to Leigh. Fitted with forty-eight-seat bodywork supplied by Roe, six of the batch – Nos 31, 32, 40-42 and 44 – had their front ends rebuilt between 1950 and 1955. The unrebuilt examples (along with rebuilt Nos 31 and 40) were withdrawn in 1956 with the exception of Nos 33, 35, 37 and 45 that survived until 1958 alongside the remaining rebuilt vehicles. *R.L. Wilson/Online Transport Archive*

The last day of operation was also the last day of South Lancashire Transport as it was officially absorbed by Lancashire United Transport. This resulted in a curious historical anomaly on 1 September 1958 when No 71 – the highest numbered trolleybus – performed a farewell ceremonial duty from Atherton to Leigh lettered 'Lancashire United Transport' – it was probably the only occasion when a new trolleybus legal operator started and closed on the same day!

Above: **Between 1936** and 1938 SLT purchased twelve Leyland TTBs – Nos 48-59 – with Roe sixty-four-seat bodywork. Of these, Nos 48-51 were acquired for Bolton Corporation (which paid for the running costs and loan charges; in 1944, when fully depreciated, the quartet became the corporation's property). These were the last of the Roe-bodied vehicles to have the extended front as evinced by No 48 – seen here in 1950 – although this particular vehicle was to have its front end rebuilt four years later (the remaining three operated unaltered through their career). The Bolton-owned examples were withdrawn in 1956. *R.L. Wilson/Online Transport Archive*

Opposite above: **The following** two batches of Roe-bodied Leyland TTBs were all owned by the company. Nos 52 and 53 were new in 1937 and Nos 54-59 the following year. Pictured in Bolton on 21 August 1958 is No 54; all eight of the company-owned vehicles survived until 1958. *C. Carter/Online Transport Archive*

Opposite below: **During the** war, SLT was allocated two batches of Utility-bodied Karrier Ws; Nos 60-63 were new in 1943. All had fifty-six-seat bodywork supplied by Weymann. Typical of the first batch is No 63, pictured here in Atherton, which, like the other three, retained its Utility bodywork until withdrawal in 1958. *Harry Luff/Online Transport Archive*

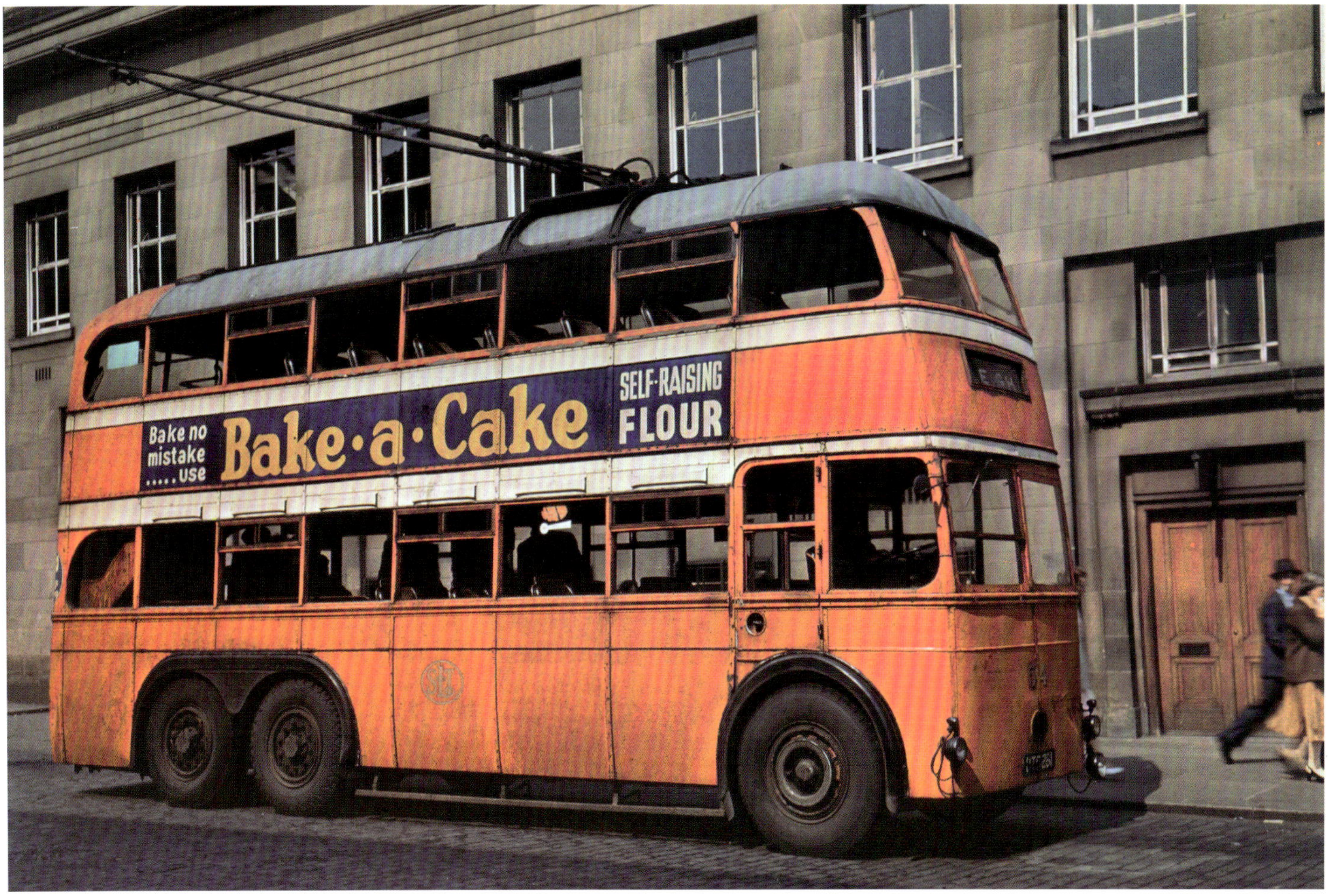
Bake no
mistake
.....use
Bake·a·Cake
SELF-RAISING
FLOUR

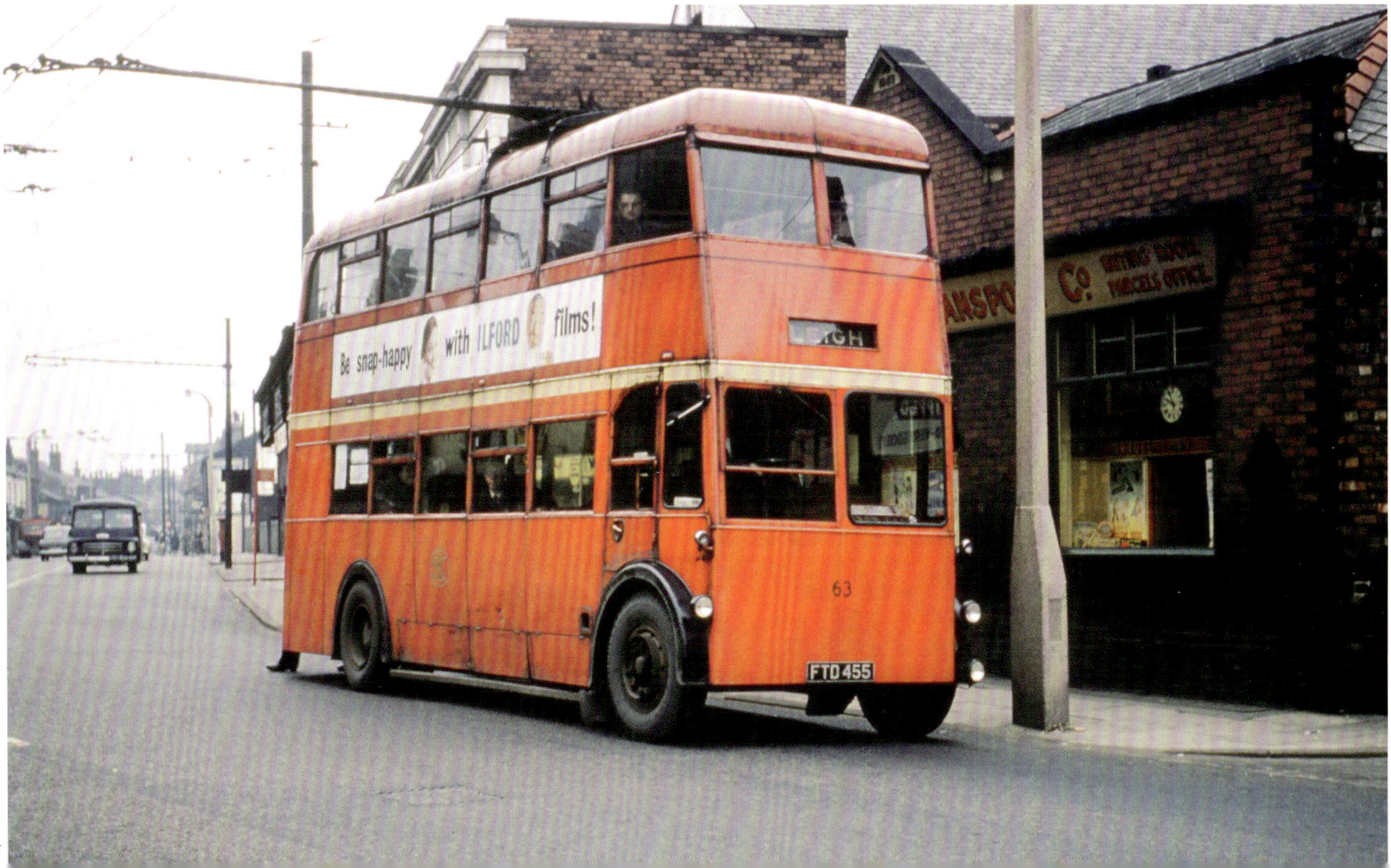
Be snap-happy with ILFORD films!
FTD 455
63

Also pictured in Atherton is No 64; this was one of the duo of Karrier Ws supplied during 1944. It and No 65 were also withdrawn during 1958. *Harry Luff/Online Transport Archive*

The only trolleybuses acquired by SLT post-war were six Sunbeam MSC2s – Nos 66-71 – new during 1947 and 1948. Fitted with Weymann sixty-four-seat bodywork, the six remained in service until 1958 with No 71 eventually being the official last trolleybus on 1 September 1958, when it ran between Atherton and Leigh. Pictured in Howell Croft bus station, Bolton, on 20 August 1958 is No 67. The local services in Bolton were converted to corporation-operated bus services on 25 March 1956 – the first SLT abandonment – but the through service to Leigh continued until 31 August 1958. *C. Carter/Online Transport Archive*

SOUTH LANCASHIRE TRANSPORT

Fleet number	Registration	Chassis	Body	New	Withdrawn	Notes
1-10	TF2072-2081	Guy BTX	Roe L60R; reseated to L56R by 1931	1930	1956-58	5, 6, 8 and 10 had rebuilt fronts 1950-55; 1 and 7 rebuilt 1953
11-30	TF5792/573/5240/ 5794-5796/5241/ 5797-5808/6951	Guy BTX	Roe L60R; reseated to L56R by 1932	1931	1955-58	11, 12, 14, 16-18, 22-25, 27-20 had fronts rebuilt 1950-55
31-46	TJ3320-3330/2969/ 3331/3332/3334/ 3335	Guy BT	Roe L48R	1933	1956-58	31, 32, 40-42, 44 had fronts rebuilt 1950-55
47	JW5370	Guy BTX	Guy H56R	1931	1951	Ex-demonstrator; acquired 1935
48-51	ATE792-795	Leyland TTB	Roe H64R	1936	1956	
52 and 53	BTE951/952	Leyland TTB	Roe H64R	1937	1958	
54-59	DTC262-266	Leyland TTB	Roe H64R	1938	1958	
60-63	FTD452-455	Karrier W	Weymann UH56R	1943	1958	
64 and 65	FTE152/153	Karrier W	Weymann UH56R	1944	1958	
66-71	HTD863-868	Sunbeam MS2	Weymann H64R	1948	1958	

Route number	From	To	Date Opened	Date Closed	Notes
	Atherton	Ashton-in-Makerfield	3 August 1930	31 August 1958	
	Atherton	Haydock	21 June 1931	11 November 1956	Through service to St Helens commenced same day; short workings operated to Hindley Green, Hindley and Ashton-in-Makerfield
	Atherton	Farnworth	19 August 1931	31 August 1958	Loops or trolley reversers were provided at Worsley, Walkden, Tyldesley, Mosley Common, Boothstown Swinton and Sandhole Colliery for short workings
	Bolton	Leigh	17 December 1933	31 August 1958	Bolton local service ceased on 25 March 1956, being replaced by a corporation-operated bus service; official last trolleybus operated 1 September 1958 from Atherton to Leigh
	Farnworth terminal loop		1936	31 August 1958	

SOUTH SHIELDS

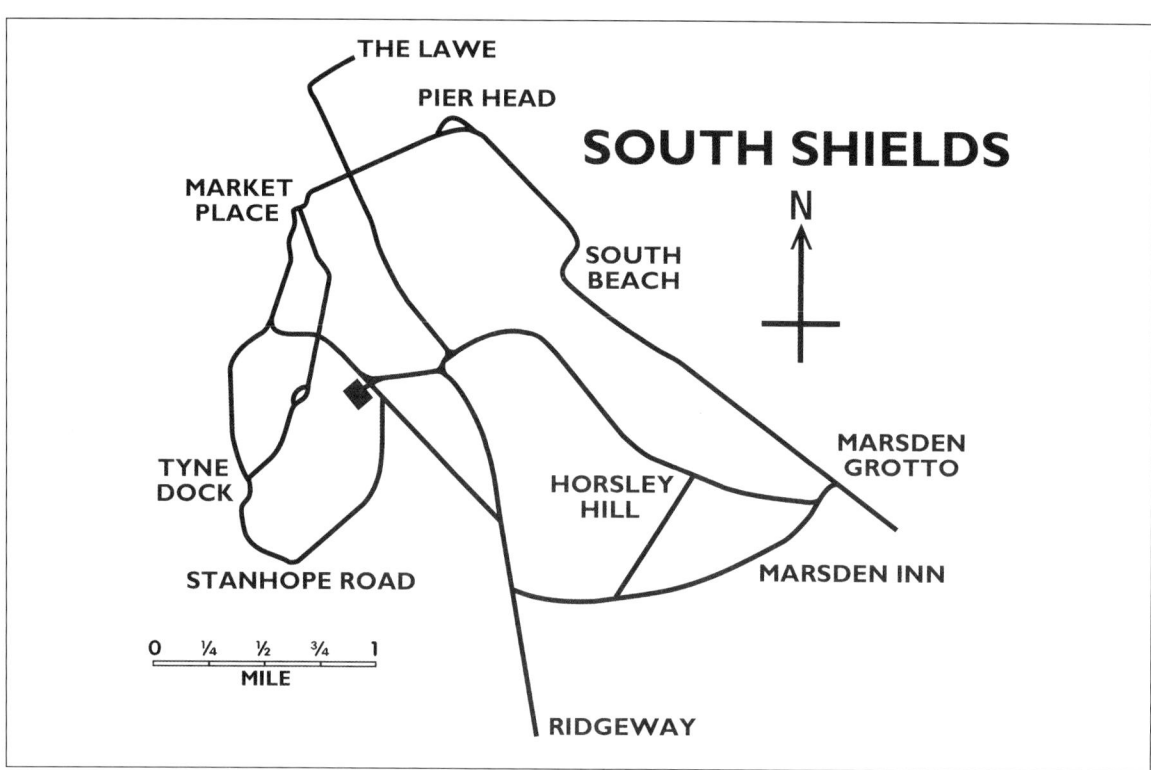

By the early 1930s, South Shields possessed a network of standard gauge trams operating over some 7½ route miles; the last extensions – including the Cleadon Light Railway to Cleadon Ridgeway – had opened in 1922 and the corporation had supplemented its existing fleet through the judicious purchase of a number of second-hand trams in the late 1920s and early 1930s. In 1936 the corporation took delivery of a new streamlined centre-entrance tram – No 52 – that was amongst the most modern to see service in north-east England. The tram seemed to have a secure future in the town.

South Shields, like a number of other towns and cities, faced the issue of providing public transport to new housing estates that were not covered by existing tramway services. The cost of extending the tramways – given the economic conditions of the early 1930s – were uneconomic and so alternatives were sought.

The period also coincided with the forced resignation of the general manager following allegations of irregularities; he was replaced by Eric Fitzpayne, the son of Frederick Andrew Fitzpayne, the general manager at Edinburgh (who died in harness in March 1935). Although Fitzpayne was to remain at South Shields for only a year, before returning to Scotland (where he ultimately became general manager at Glasgow), during his tenure, on 6 June 1934, the corporation decided to seek powers to operate trolleybuses. Having missed the opportunity to get a Bill deposited in the 1934 parliamentary session, a Bill was presented the following session and, on 2 August 1935, the South Shields Corporation Act 1935 received the Royal Assent. A second Act – the South Shields Corporation (Trolley Vehicles) Order Confirmation Act 1939 – received the Royal Assent on 13 July 1939.

Although the original Act empowered the corporation to introduce trolleybuses to routes not previously served by tram, crucially it also permitted the conversion of the tram routes to trolleybus. The initial trolleybus route – from the Market Place to Fremantle Road via Laygate and Chichester – was largely a new service and designed to serve some of the new housing; this service, for which four trolleybuses were ordered from Karrier, was inaugurated on 12 October 1936 with work on erecting the overhead having started six months earlier. Whilst this work was in progress, the future of the tram service from Pier Head to Stanhope Road Top via Laygate and Tyne Dock was under consideration; the track was life expired, and the corporation decided to replace it with trolleybuses. With the success of the new trolleybus services the corporation decided on the replacement of its entire tramway system – with the exception of the service to Cleadon Ridgeway – by trolleybus. The Pier Head to Stanhope Road Top service, for which a further four trolleybuses were acquired, commenced operation on 11 April 1937. Three days later, the trolleybus service from Ocean Road to Chichester – which ran alongside the tram service to Cleadon Ridgeway for much of its route – was introduced. A further twenty-seven trolleybuses were acquired during 1937 and 1938 for the conversion work. Apart from the Cleadon Ridgeway service all the tram routes had now

Between 1936 and 1938, South Shields took delivery of thirty-four Karrier E4s fitted with Weymann fifty-six-seat bodywork. The first four – Nos 200-03 – arrived in 1936 with the remainder following over the next two years. Two of the batch – Nos 203 and 231 – were destroyed during an air raid in September 1931 and were subsequently rebodied. The introduction of route numbers in 1950 resulted in the slight modification of the front – as evinced by No 210 seen here in this view taken at Market Place with the Old Town Hall (completed in 1768) in the background – although the first four of the batch had been withdrawn by the end of that year. Six remained operational until 1963 and one of these – No 204 – was preserved on withdrawal. *Harry Luff/Online Transport Archive*

In 1942, South Shields acquired two second-hand vehicles in order to supplement its fleet to cope with wartime demand. The first of this duo was ex-Bradford No 633 which became South Shields No 235. Based around the AEC 'Q' type bus chassis and designated Model 761T, No 633 had been displayed at the 1933 Commercial Motor Show and had arrived in Bradford as a demonstrator before being purchased. The trolleybus acquired the nickname 'Queenie' whilst in service in the West Riding. Fitted with an English Electric sixty-three-seat body, the prevailing restrictions, which limited two-axle vehicles to a maximum length of 26ft, meant that the chassis had virtually no rear overhang – a fact emphasised in this view of No 235 from the back. The production of AEC 761Ts was limited with only five being constructed during 1933 and 1934. No 235 was to survive in operation on Tyneside until in 1951. *J. Joyce Collection/ Online Transport Archive*

been converted; in order to operate the one surviving tram service, thirteen trams were retained (out of the forty-nine operated at the system's peak).

This was followed on 2 May 1937 by the extension, not previously served by tram, of the Fremantle Road service to Marsden Bay and, on 3 May 1937, by the conversion of the tram route from Chichester to Stanhope Road Top. The following year saw the opening of the long coast route from Pier Head to Marsden Grotto in two stages: from Pier Head to South Beach on 9 July 1938 and thence to Marsden Bay, where it connected into the route from Fremantle Road, a fortnight later. The Marsden Bay service was extended to Marsden Grotto on 22 July 1939. Between 1941 and 1944, as a result of the Second World War, services along the coastal route were suspended. However, in order to provide a useful cross-town service linking the housing estates with the docks, two extensions were opened on 28 September 1942; these were from Horsley Hill Square to Prince Edward Street, close to the original Fremantle Road terminus, and from Laygate to Tyne Dock via Temple Town. In order to supplement its fleet during the war, South Shields acquired five second-hand trolleybuses, four from Bradford and a Thornycroft single-decker from Bournemouth; No 236 was the only single-deck trolleybus to be

The second of the pair of second-hand trolleybuses acquired in 1942 was obtained from Bournemouth and was the only single-deck trolleybus to be operated by South Shields Corporation. No 236 was a Thornycroft BD fitted with a Brush-built thirty-two-seat body and had been new originally to Bournemouth – where again it was the only single-deck trolleybus to see service – in 1933. It was to be withdrawn finally in 1950. *J. Joyce Collection/Online Transport Archive*

operated by the corporation. During the war, South Shields suffered damage on a number of occasions; during a raid on 30 September, Nos 203, 231 and 234 had their original bodies destroyed in Market Square; all returned to service rebodied the following year.

During 1945 and 1946, a batch of six Utility-bodied Karrier Ws were delivered. On 31 March 1946, South Shields bade farewell to its trams with the conversion of the service to Cleadon Ridgeway; this required the erection of two sections of overhead – from Sunderland Road to King George Road and from King George Road to the terminus – as much of the route was already equipped with trolleybus overhead from earlier conversions.

Further extensions in 1947 – from Laygate Lane to Station Road via Commercial Road and from Mile End Road to The Lawe (both on 24 July) and in 1948 – from Westoe to Marsden Inn via Horsley Hill Square (in two stages on 5 January and 28 March) – took the system to its maximum extent of some 16 route miles. In order to operate the new services a total of twenty-five new trolleybuses were delivered between 1947 and 1950; their arrival allowed for the withdrawal of the second-hand vehicles acquired during the war. Nos 261-70 were also the last new trolleybuses delivered to the corporation; subsequent purchases between 1957 and 1959 were second-hand from Pontypridd and St Helens and resulted in the demise of a number of the pre-war Karriers. The entire fleet was housed, throughout its history, in the corporation's two depots at Dean Road, Chichester. The first of these had opened with the electric tramway in 1906; the second followed in 1925.

In the early 1950s, route numbers were introduced for the first time; there were a number of interlinked services and the route numbers were as follows:

1. Pier Head to Stanhope Road Top via Westoe and Chichester (linked between Tyne Dock and Stanhope Road Top as a circular service with route 2)
2. Pier Head to Tyne Dock via Market Place and Laygate (linked between Tyne Dock and Stanhope Road Top as a circular service with route 1)
3. Market Place to Tyne Dock via Fowler Street, Westoe and Laygate (linked between Tyne Dock and Stanhope Road Top with route 4 to form a figure of eight)

Continuing vehicle shortages resulted in South Shields returning to Bradford in 1945 to purchase a further three second-hand trolleybuses; they retained their original Bradford blue livery for their brief sojourn on Tyneside. Nos 237-39 were a trio of English Electric E11s fitted with the same manufacturer's fifty-six-seat bodywork that dated originally to 1930-32. Due to issues with their outdated control equipment and height, they were largely restricted to use on the route from Prince Edward Road to Fremantle Road. No 237 – illustrated here – had originally been Bradford No 582 and had entered service in the West Riding in March 1930. The arrival of Nos 240-45 during 1945 and 1946 rendered the ex-Bradford vehicles quickly surplus to requirements and they were withdrawn in 1946 (No 237) and 1947 (Nos 238 and 239). *J.S. King/via Philip Hanson Collection/Online Transport Archive*

4. Market Place to Stanhope Road Top via Laygate and Chichester(linked between Tyne Dock and Stanhope Road Top with route 3 to form a figure of eight)
5. The Lawe to Cleadon Ridgeway
7. Market Place to Horsley Hill via King George Road and Centenary Avenue
8. Tyne Dock to Horsley Hill via Chichester and Centenary Avenue
9. Tyne Dock to The Lawe via Trinity Church and Market Place
10. Marsden Grotto to Stanhope Road Top via South Beach, Pier Head, Market Place and Tyne Dock
11. Market Place to Marsden Grotto via Chichester, Prince Edward Road and Marsden Inn
12. Market Place to Marsden Grotto via Westoe, Highfield Road and Marsden Inn

After the expansion of the period between 1946 and 1948, the network remained largely unchanged for almost a decade. However, the financial performance of the route from Pier Head to Marsden Grotto via South Beach was not strong and this was compounded by problems of maintenance in a coastal environment. During 1957, therefore, as much of the equipment required replacement, it was decided to convert the route to bus operation.

Pictured at the Pier Head terminus, adjacent to the Wouldhave Monument, on 28 June 1952, prior to heading to Tyne Dock with a service on route 2 is Karrier W No 245; this was the last of a batch of six delivered during 1945 and 1946 that were the first new trolleybuses supplied after the Second World War to the corporation. Fitted with Roe-built fifty-six-seat bodywork, the six were withdrawn between 1962 and 1964. *John Meredith/Online Transport Archive*

The first conversion saw buses introduced to the section from South Beach to Marsden Bay on 10 February 1958 was unscheduled, however, but prompted by heavy snow three days earlier that had disrupted the trolleybus service. The remainder of the route, from Pier Head to South Beach, was converted in late 1962.

In 1959, the general manager produced a report advocating the replacement of the remaining trolleybuses by motorbus; his argument was not financial but of flexibility, commenting on the need to provide 'an elastic transport system capable of expansion to meet new needs, and in this respect the trolleybuses are at an obvious disadvantage'. In October 1959, the corporation decided to implement a conversion policy but defer its commencement – other than for the immediate withdrawal of service 9 (which did not result in the reduction to the overhead as it was effectively a workmen's service) – for a two-year period.

The first route to be converted was the long route from The Lawe to Cleadon Ridgeway; as a result of road improvements, this route was converted on 2 October 1961 although the only sections of overhead removed at this stage were the short section from Mile End Road to The Lawe and from King George Road to the terminus as again all other sections were covered by alternative routes.

The final new trolleybuses acquired by South Shields came in two batches of Karriers; the first ten – Nos 251-60 – were new during 1947 and 1948. These were W4 chassis fitted with Northern Coachbuilders fifty-six-seat bodywork. No 259 is seen in the Market Place prior to heading towards the Pier Head. During early 1964, the number of operational trolleybuses declined as additional motorbuses were introduced with both types operating alongside each other on the surviving routes. By April, only twelve trolleybuses were still in service and one of this batch – No 260 – was destined to operate the last journey from Pier Head to Stanhope Road on the final day. *Harry Luff/Online Transport Archive*

Also recorded at the Pier Head terminus on 28 June 1952 is No 262. This was one of a batch of ten Karrier F4s fitted with Northern Coachbuilders fifty-six-seat bodywork that were new in 1950; the batch represented the last new trolleybuses ordered by South Shields and were withdrawn during 1963 and 1964 during the final run down of the system. One of the batch – No 260 – operated, without any ceremony, the final trolleybus duty on 28 April 1964. *John Meredith/Online Transport Archive*

The late 1950s and early 1960s witnessed a decline in the standards of maintenance with dewirings commonplace; such was the state of the overhead that the Ministry of Transport imposed a temporary 20mph speed limit over the system for a period.

The final conversion, following the removal of the Tyne Dock to South Beach section in late 1962, came in two stages. The first – on 1 May 1963 saw the elimination of all the routes serving the south-east of the town from Chichester and Westoe. The final conversion was to come on 29 April 1964 when the complex network of routes serving Pier Head and Tyne Dock succumbed; such was the decline in the system that, by the final day, only three trolleybuses remained operational with one of these – No 260 – operating the final service without ceremony. Of the South Shields fleet only one example – No 204 (a Karrier E4 from 1937) – survives in preservation.

Following the acquisition of the ten Karrier F4s in 1950, the only additional vehicles that South Shields acquired were two batches of second-hand trolleybuses. The first of these, which entered service during 1957, were four Karrier Ws fitted with Utility fifty-six-seat bodywork built by Park Royal that had originally been Pontypridd Nos 8, 9, 12 and 13. No 234, pictured here heading towards Horsley Hill Estate, had originally been new in 1945. The four vehicles were all withdrawn during 1963. *Harry Luff/Online Transport Archive*

The last trolleybuses to enter service in South Shields were eight Sunbeam F4s with East Lancs fifty-six-seat bodywork which were acquired second-hand from St Helens and entered service during 1958 and 1959. Ex-St Helens Nos 374-81, new during 1950 and 1951, represented the only 8ft 0in wide trolleybuses to operate with South Shields. Unfortunately, their arrival coincided with a report produced by the corporation's then general manager that advocated the replacement of trolleybuses by motorbuses. As a result, the eight were not destined for a long second life, all being withdrawn during 1963. Here No 203 is pictured prior to operating a service on route 7 to Horsley Hill Estate. *Harry Luff/Online Transport Archive*

SOUTH SHIELDS • 123

Fleet number	Registration	Chassis	Body	New	Withdrawn	Notes
200-03	CU3589-3592	Karrier E4	Weymann H56R (203 rebodied by Weymann 1942; body of 200 transferred to 205 1952)	1936	1955-58	
204-07	CU9593-9596	Karrier E4	Weymann H55R (205 received body from 200 in 1952 and became 200 [ii] CY3589)	1937	1957-63	204 preserved
208-33	CU3850-3873/3974/3975	Karrier E4	Weymann H55R (231 rebodied by Weymann in 1942)	1937-38	1950-63	
234	CWK67	Daimler CTM4	Willowbrook H56R (rebodied by Weymann in 1942)	1938	1958	
235	KW6210	AEC 761T	EE H63F	1934	1951	Ex-Bradford 633; acquired 1942
236	LJ7704	Thornycroft BD	Brush B32C	1933	1950	Ex-Bournemouth 71; acquired 1942
237-39	KW6658/9459/1360	EE E11	EE H56R	1929-32	1946-47	Ex-Bradford 582/90/96; acquired 1945
240-45	CU4601-4606	Karrier W	Roe UH56R	1945-46	1962-64	
246-48	CU4716-4718	Karrier W4	NCB H56R	1947	1962-1963	
249 and 250	CU4719/4720	Karrier W4	Roe H56R	1947	1963	
251-60	CU4873-4877/4943-4947	Karrier W4	NCB H56R	1947-48	1963-64	
261-70	CU5100-5105/5279-5282	Sunbeam F4	NCB H56R	1950	1963-64	
236-39	GNY301/302, FTG234/235	Karrier W4	PR UH56R	1945-46	1963	Ex-Pontypridd 8, 9, 13 and 13; acquired 1957
201-03/05-09	BDJ74-81	Sunbeam F4	East Lancs H56R	1950-51	1963	Ex-St Helens 374-81; acquired 1958-59
Wartime loan						
79, 79, 123	AEL406-407/ALJ997	Sunbeam MS2	PR or EE H56D	1934-35	1943	Bournemouth 78, 79 and 123; had previously been loaned to Newcastle; in service with South Shields February-May 1943

Route number (see text)	From	To	Date Opened	Date Closed	Notes
	Market	Fremantle Road (via Laygate and Chichester)	12 October 1936	1 May 1963 (Chichester to Fremantle Road); 29 April 1964 (Market to Chichester)	
	Market	Pier Head	11 April 1937	29 April 1964	
	Laygate	Stanhope Road Top (via Tyne Dock)	11 April 1937	29 April 1964	
	Ocean Road	Chichester (via Westoe)	14 April 1937	29 April 1964	
	Fremantle Road	Marsden Bay	2 May 1937	1 May 1963	
	Chichester	Stanhope Road Top	3 May 1937	29 April 1964	
	Pier Head	South Beach	9 July 1938	Late 1962	
	South Beach	Marsden Bay	23 July 1938	9 February 1958	
	Marsden Bay	Marsden Grotto	22 July 1939	1 May 1963	
	Laygate	Tyne Dock (via Temple Town)	28 September 1942	29 April 1964	
	Prince Edward Road East	Horsley Hill Square	28 September 1942	1 May 1963	
	Sunderland Road	King George Road	31 March 1946	1 May 1963	
	King George Road (Prince Edward Road)	Ridgeway	31 March 1946	2 October 1961	
	Laygate Lane	Station Road (via Commercial Road)	24 July 1947	29 April 1964	
	Mile End Road	The Lawe	24 July 1947	2 October 1961	
	Westoe	Horsley Hill Square	5 January 1948	1 May 1963	
	Horsley Hill Square	Marsden Inn	28 March 1948	1 May 1963	

STOCKPORT

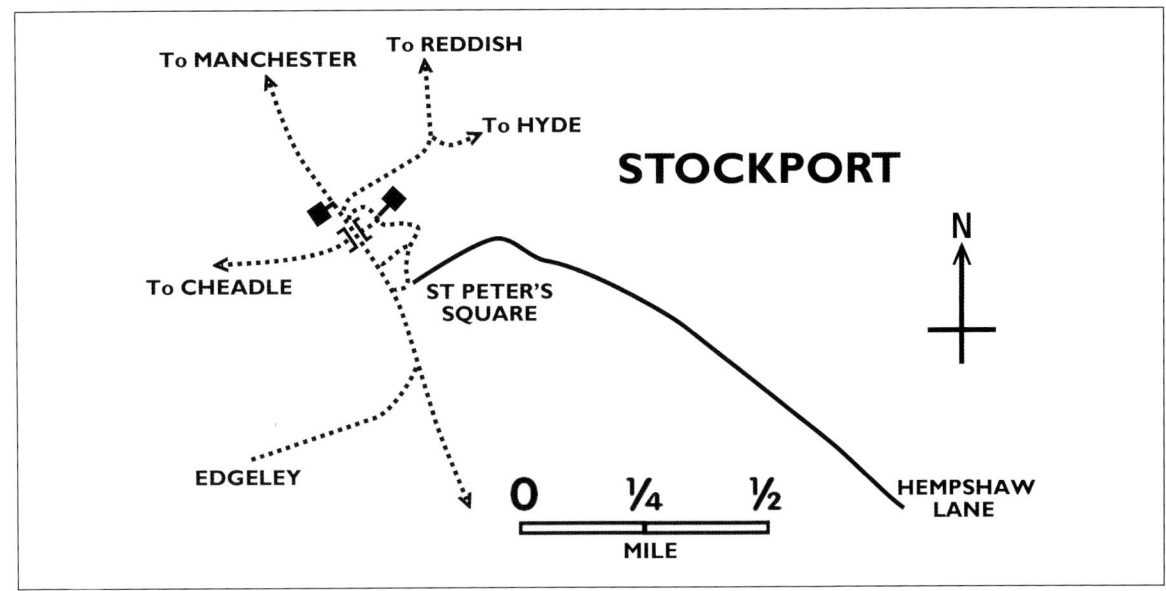

During the first decade of the twentieth century, Stockport Corporation developed a significant standard gauge tramway with through services to Manchester and over the SHMD network. There remained, however, parts of the borough that were not as yet served; these included the Offerton district.

Initially, the corporation contemplated extending the tramway to serve Offerton and the Marple UDC beyond but the costs proved prohibitive and so an alternative solution was sought. The initial trolleybus routes had opened in Bradford and Leeds in June 1911 and, following an inspective of these plus a trip to Bremen to see trolleybuses in operation there, it was decided to adopt trolleybuses for the new route.

The visit to Germany proved highly significant as Bremen had adopted the Lloyd-Kohler system of overhead. This system, unlike the overhead adopted in Bradford and Leeds (as well as the Cedes-Stoll system), used two parallel wires suspended vertically rather than horizontally. Only one set of wires was necessary with the vehicles exchanging conductor gear when they met (which did replicate the operation on the Cedes-Stoll system). The overhead system – known locally as 'the monkey' – was prone to failure, causing disruption to the service (and other road users).

Although there were plans to extend the route beyond the borough boundary, neither Marple nor Hazel Grove UDCs were willing to contribute to the cost with the result that the route, when it opened on 10 March 1913, extended the 1¾ miles from St Peter's Square along Offerton Road to Hemphaw Lane.

For the new service, three single-deckers were supplied by Brush, with the chassis being based on 3-4ton CC model chassis supplied by Daimler; these were based at the corporation's tram depot in Mersey Square. Nos 1-3 were the first British trolleybuses

Stockport Corporation adopted the unique – for Britain – Lloyd-Kohler equipment for its overhead. This – like the Cedes-Stoll system – was European in origin and, during the First World War, spare parts proved impossible to obtain. One of the three all-Brush trolleybuses was sold to Mexborough & Swinton in 1916. Post-war, the trolleybus service was intermittent, with the remaining two vehicles often out of action requiring repair and the service ceased entirely on 11 September 1920. Pre its sale in 1916, No 1 is seen here on Offerton Road exchanging trolleys with No 2. The corporation's sole route – from St Peter's Square to the borough boundary at Hempshaw Lane – was about 1¾ miles in length. *Harry Luff Collection/Online Transport Archive*

built with pedal control – rather than the traditional tram controller used in earlier examples – thus freeing the driver to use both hands on the steering wheel.

The outbreak of the First World War in August 1914 posed a serious problem for the operator as spare parts became almost impossible to obtain. In 1916, one of the three vehicles was sold to Mexborough & Swinton, whilst the remaining two soldiered on. By 1919 the operational fleet had been reduced to one and when that suffered from a broken rear axle – a regular problem with the trio – on 17 June 1919, all trolleybus services were temporarily suspended.

Although the trolleybus service was restored, it only operated sporadically thereafter and all operation ceased on 11 September 1920.

Fleet number	Registration	Chassis	Body	New	Withdrawn	Notes
1-3	N/A	Daimler-Brush	Brush B29R	1913	1916-20	1 sold to Mexborough & Swinton in 1916

Route number	From	To	Date Opened	Date Closed	Notes
N/A	Town Centre (St Peter's Square)	Hempshaw Lane	10 March 1913	11 September 1920	

WEST HARTLEPOOL

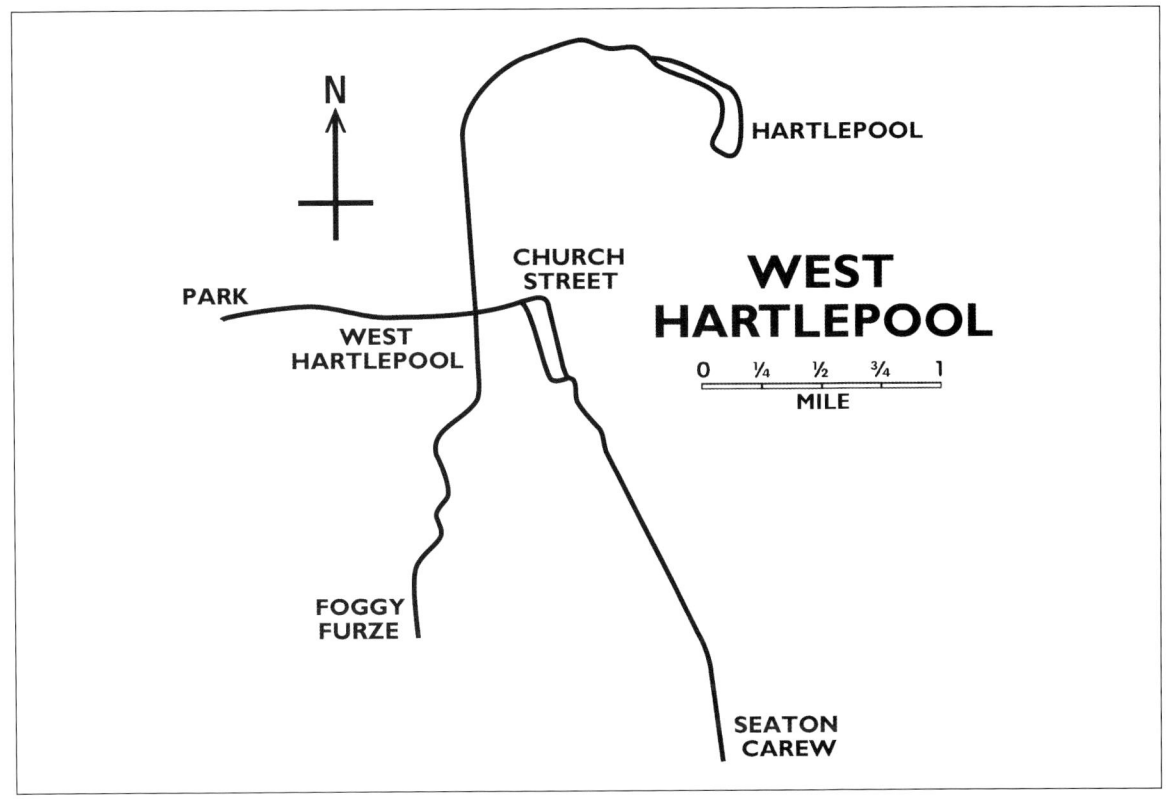

It was not until 1 April 1967 that Hartlepool and West Hartlepool were combined into a single entity – the County Borough of Hartlepool – and the split between the two until that point was to affect the development of public transport in the district.

Between 1884 and 1891, 3ft 6in gauge steam trams operated between Hartlepool and West Hartlepool. In 1895 the moribund track was acquired by the General Electric Tramways Co Ltd, a subsidiary of the Electric Construction Co, and the line was reopened with electric traction on 19 May 1896. A second company the Hartlepool Electric Tramways Co Ltd, a subsidiary of BET, was established; this opened routes to Park and Foggy Furze and, in 1899, following BET's purchase of the General Electric Tramways Co, both tramways were united under single ownership. A final tram route – to Seaton Carew – was opened on 28 March 1902. This took the system to almost exactly seven route miles; of this the vast bulk was in West Hartlepool but a section and the Cleveland Road depot were in Hartlepool.

On 31 August 1912, West Hartlepool exercised its powers and acquired the tramways within its boundaries; this left the section within Hartlepool itself still in company ownership – where it remained until 1925 – with the corporation operating services on the through route with a lease on that section.

For the opening of the West Hartlepool system on 27 February 1924, Railless supplied four single-deck trolleybuses – Nos 1-4 – that were fitted with Short bodywork. In this posed view, designed to demonstrate the flexibility of this new form of transport, No 3 is pictured overtaking an LGOC-built tower wagon. The Foggy Furze route, which had been tram operated until October 1923, had seen bus operation pending the introduction of the new trolleybuses. This route was the first on the system to be converted to bus operation – on 15 October 1938 – despite the recent acquisition of new double-deck trolleybuses and proposals for the extension of the route to connect with that to Seaton Carew. The tower wagon was originally LGOC No B2766 and was acquired by West Hartlepool in 1920; it was sold for scrap in 1929. *Hartlepool Corporation Transport/John Meredith Collection/Online Transport Archive*

By the early 1920s, the condition of the tramway – particularly the route to Foggy Furze – was giving some cause for concern and the costs of repair were considered excessive. It was decided, after visiting the existing systems in Bradford, Leeds and Rotherham, to introduce trolleybuses. Powers for the abandonment of the tramways and their conversion to trolleybus operation was enshrined in the West Hartlepool Corporation Act, which received its Royal Assent on 2 August 1923.

The first stage of the conversion occurred on 4 October 1923 when motorbuses temporarily replaced the trams on the Foggy Furze service. Work then progressed on the conversion of the route, which was extended by two-thirds of a mile to Upper Church Street, and the first four trolleybuses were delivered. Following the official inspection on 27 February 1924, public services commenced the following day (although heavy snow caused problems with adhesion). The vehicles were all based at the Cleveland Road depot, which they accessed through the use of a skate and the tram track and overhead.

The new system – despite the snow – was successful and in early 1925 it was decided to convert the route to Park. Tram services over the section ceased in November 1925 with the new trolleybuses being introduced on 4 February 1926.

Contemporaneously, the future of the through tramway was becoming important. The company's ownership of the section in Hartlepool was due to expire on 2 August 1925 and, the previous year, discussions had commenced between the company and the two corporations as to the route's future. West Hartlepool favoured trolleybuses; Hartlepool favoured buses. Eventually a compromise was reached, and Hartlepool duly took over ownership of the section of track within its boundaries. As a result of the Hartlepool Corporation (Trolley Vehicles) Act, which received the Royal Assent on 30 June 1926, the corporation was empowered to convert the tramway within its boundaries to trolleybus operation. Although the system was operated thereafter by West Hartlepool, the vehicles used on the joint route were nominally owned by both with each corporation sharing half the revenue and half the operating costs.

Tramway operation on the through route ceased on 22 February 1927, with Lt-Col H. Mount having undertaken the statutory inspection of the new trolleybus route earlier in the month, with the trolleybuses taking over on the following day. This left only one tram route – that to Seaton Carew – and this last operated on 25 March 1927; the new trolleybuses took over the following day.

By the mid-1930s, the future of the system was under consideration particularly as the fleet was increasingly aged and out of date. The then Sunderland general manager, C.A. Hopkins (who had undertaken a major modernisation of the Sunderland tramway system), was appointed as a consultant. His recommendations included a number of extensions and the purchase of new vehicles. Powers to construct the new routes were enshrined in a Provisional Order obtained in 1938. One of these involved linking the Seaton Carew route with that to Foggy Furze via Seaton Lane; this involved a low railway bridge. As a result, three new single-deckers – Nos 7-9 – were acquired in 1939; these were destined to be the last trolleybuses purchased for the system.

However, Nos 7-9 were not to see service on the route for which they were intended, as the extension was never completed and, pending work on the new route, motorbuses replaced trolleybuses – in theory temporarily – on the Foggy Furze route on 15 October

The first double-deck trolleybuses acquired by West Hartlepool, after the short-lived No 7 of 1927, were a batch of six – Nos 1-6 – that were supplied by Daimler in May 1938. Fitted with Roe bodywork, the six were to survive until the final conversion of the system to bus operation in 1953. Here No 6 is pictured outside the system's depot at Cleveland Road. *W.J. Wyse*

1938; trolleybuses were never reintroduced and the overhead was removed. There was one extension opened that year, however, when the terminus in Hartlepool was extended from Trinity Church to form a one-way loop via Middlegate (although it remained possible to turn trolleybuses at the original terminus through the use of gravity as the overhead had been removed).

After the war, the future of the system was again under consideration; this was partly the result of the age of the feeder cables from the power station at Burn Road, where the cost of replacement, and the fact that West Hartlepool had developed a significant motorbus operation. In a reversal of the positions in the early 1920s, West Hartlepool now favoured the motorbus and Hartlepool the trolleybus. In the summer of 1946 West Hartlepool decided to convert the system; an order for two new trolleybuses was cancelled in favour of one for additional motorbuses but work on conversion was not immediately progressed; indeed, some sections of overhead were renewed.

It was not until 1949 that the first steps towards final conversion commenced. The Seaton Carew service was converted on 18 November 1949, although it was not until February 1951 that the route's overhead was removed. This conversion was followed on 7 March 1953 by the service to Park.

The finale of trolleybus operation was marked by an element of the local rivalry that had been a hallmark of the operation periodically throughout its history. West Hartlepool decided to terminate the agreement for the joint operation of the through route and both corporations successfully obtained licences to operate the service. The last trolleybuses operated – without ceremony – on 2 April 1953; the next day the replacement motorbus service was operated exclusively by West Hartlepool; it was not until 1 August 1953 when vehicles operated on behalf of Hartlepool Corporation by Bee-Line Roadways first made their appearance. The beauty of local politics and rivalry writ large!

A second batch of Daimler CTM4s – Nos 32-39 – was delivered later in 1938; ownership of these was shared between Hartlepool and West Hartlepool corporations. These were acquired to replace the single-deckers that had been used on the joint service between the two towns following its introduction on 23 February 1927. These again survived until the system's final conversion in April 1953. *W.J. Wyse*

Fleet number	Registration	Chassis	Body	New	Withdrawn	Notes
1-4	EF2121-2124	Railless	Short B36F	1924	1930	
5 and 6	EF3025-3026	Railless	Short B36C	1926	1937-38	
7	EF3027	Railless	Short O48RO	1926	1928	
8-19	EF3358-3369	Straker-Clough LL	Vickers B32C	1927	1937-40	Jointly owned with Hartlepool Council
20-31	EF3370-3381	Garrett O	Roe B32C	1927	1937-39	
1-6	EF6701-6706	Daimler CTM4	Roe H53R	1938	1953	
32-39	EF6892-6899	Daimler CTM4	Roe H53R	1938	1953	Jointly owned with Hartlepool Council
7-9	EF7037-7039	Leyland TB7	Roe B32C	1939	1950	

Route number	From	To	Date Opened	Date Closed	Notes
	Church Street	Foggy Furze	27 February 1924	14 October 1938	
	Church Street	Park	4 February 1926	7 March 1953	
	Church Street	Trinity Church, Hartlepool	23 February 1927	2 April 1953	Extended to Middlegate 1938 and original loop abandoned
	Church Street	Seaton Carew	28 March 1927	18 November 1949	
	Trinity Church, Hartlepool	Middlegate, Hartlepool	1938	2 April 1953	

On 24 August 1951 Daimler CTM4 No 32 – one of the batch of eight jointly owned by West Hartlepool and Hartlepool corporations – stands on Church Street in Hartlepool. In the background can be seen the Hartlepool depot of the United Automobile Co. *C. Carter/Online Transport Archive*

WIGAN

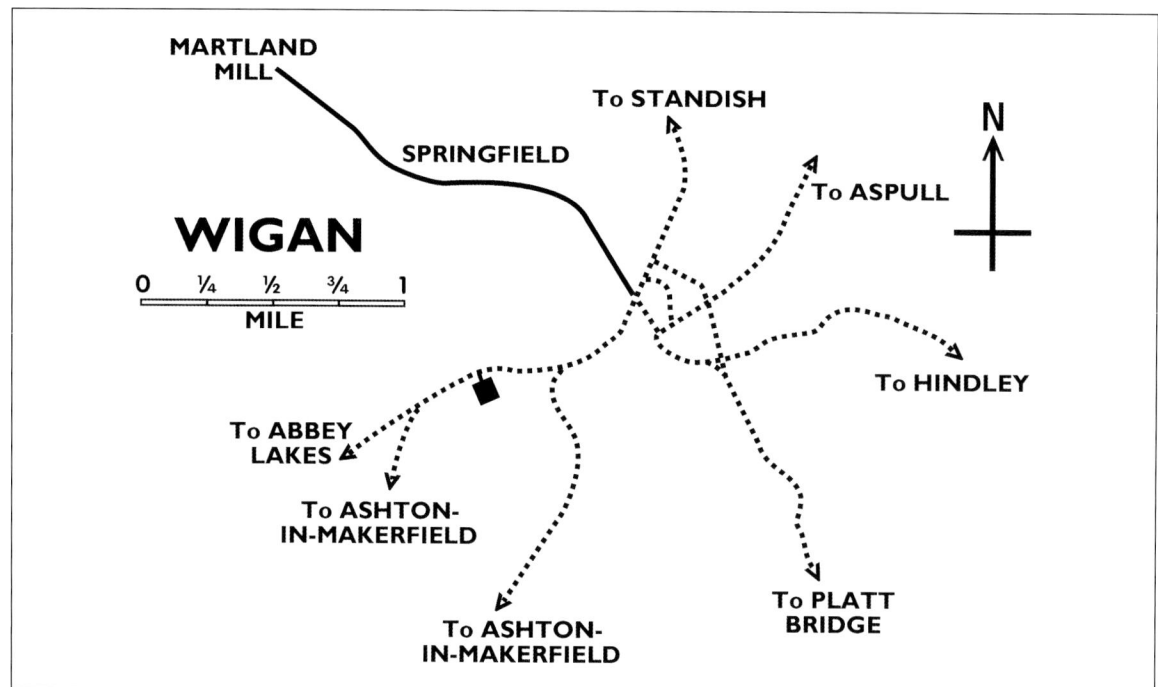

Wigan Corporation acquired in 1902 a network of 3ft 6in gauge tramways from the Wigan & District Tramways Co; the corporation had already decided to convert these to electric traction and extend the network again using 3ft 6in trams. However, the narrow gauge was atypical in the area and, eventually, the corporation decided to adopt 4ft 8½in instead for newer lines and convert the older routes to standard gauge.

By the early 1920s, the majority of the network had been converted and, following the conversion within the borough boundary of the Aspull route in December 1923 (the section beyond the boundary was converted to bus operation), only one section – the 1½-mile route from the town centre to Martland Mill – remained 3ft 6in.

The costs of converting the route, which was not a great success financially, was estimated at £30,000 and that, following research, replacement by trolleybuses would cost about one-third of that amount. Motorbuses were also examined; however, the number of stops served plus the hilly nature of the route with the consequent need to purchase more powerful buses meant that their operation was perceived as significantly more costly.

In mid-1924, the corporation decided to replace the trams with trolleybuses and ordered four single-deckers for the purpose. Curiously, the corporation never actually obtained formal powers to operate trolleybuses, although did consider doing so.

For its trolleybus service, Wigan Corporation acquired four Brush-bodied single-deckers through the contractors Clough, Smith & Co Ltd; the quartet had chassis supplied by Straker-Squire Ltd of Edmonton in London. All four – Nos 1-4 – were delivered during May 1925 and were originally fitted with solid tyres. In 1929, the four were – uniquely – equipped with pneumatic tyres on the front axle only in order to reduce vibration as seen in this view. The problems caused by solid tyres on poor road surfaces were encountered by a number of earlier trolleybus operators and undoubtedly led to many of these pioneering systems having short operational lives. The four Wigan trolleybuses were all withdrawn following the abandonment of the system at the end of September 1930. *Geoff Lumb Collection*

The conversion of the route took place in May 1925, with the town centre provided with a loop at the corner of Market Street and Woodcock Street and a triangular reverser at Martland Mill. A loop was also provided for short workings at Springfield. The four trolleybuses were accommodated at the corporation's Melverley Street depot; this was about a mile from the town centre and was accessed by the trolleybuses using the tram overhead and a skate on the track.

From the late 1920s, the corporation started the process of converting its surviving tram routes. Although there were plans for the expansion of the trolleybus network including routes to Ashton-in-Makerfield and Hindley where connections into the South Lancashire Transport system would have enabled through services to operate, these plans came to nought and motorbuses were employed to replace the trams.

The final trams operated on 28 March 1931; this left the small trolleybus system exposed as track and overhead had to be maintained to permit access to the depot. As a consequence, the trolleybuses were soon replaced; the last services operated on 30 September 1931.

Fleet number	Registration	Chassis	Body	New	Withdrawn	Notes
1-4	EK2967-3970	Straker Squire	Brush B37C	1925	1931	

Route number	From	To	Date Opened	Date Closed	Notes
N/A	Town Centre (Market Street)	Martland Mill	7 May 1925	30 September 1931	

BIBLIOGRAPHY

Barker, Colin, et al; 'Trolleybus Classics' series; Middleton Press; 1995 onwards
Brook, Roy; *The Trolleybuses of Huddersfield*; MTMS; 1976
Buses Illustrated/Buses; Ian Allan Ltd; since 1949
Canneaux, T.P, and Hanson, N.H.; *The Trolleybuses of Newcastle upon Tyne 1936-1966 (Second Edition)*; Newcastle upon Tyne City Libraries; 1985
Deans, Brian; *Glasgow's Trolleybuses*; *Scottish Tramway Museum Society*; 1972
Deans, Brian, and Little, Stuart; *Glasgow Trolleybuses*; Trolleybooks; 2020
Eyre, D.M., Heaps, C.W., and Taylor, C.; *Manchester's Trolleybuses*; MTMS; 1967
Eyre, Michael, and Heaps, Chris; *The Manchester Trolleybus*; Ian Allan Publishing; 2008
Griffiths, Geoff; *Llanelly Trolleybuses*; Trolleybooks; 1992
Hyde, W.G.S.; *A History of Public Transport in Ashton-under-Lyne*; MTMS; 1980
Joyce, J., King, J. S. and Newman, A. G.; *British Trolleybus Systems*; Ian Allan Ltd; 1986
Joyce, J.; *Trolleybus Trails*; Ian Allan Ltd; 1963
King, J.S.; *Keighley Corporation Transport*; Advertiser Press; 1964
King, Stanley; *Bradford Trolleybuses*; Venture Publications; 1994
Kraemer-Johnson, Glyn, and Bishop, John; *Trolleybus Memories: Brighton*; Ian Allan Publishing; 2007
Lockwood, Stephen; A-Z of British Trolleybuses; The Crowood Press; 2017
Lumb, Geoff; *Ian Allan Transport Library: British Trolleybuses 1911-1972*; Ian Allan Ltd; 1995
Maybin, Mike; *Belfast Trolleybuses*; Trolleybooks; 2015
Maybin, Mike; *A Nostalgic Look at Belfast Trolleybuses 1938-1968*; Silver Link; 1996
Owen, Nicholas; *History of the British Trolleybus*; David & Charles; 1974
Sandford, Geoffrey; *The Trolleybuses of St Helens*; Reading Transport Society; undated
Symons, R.D.H., and Creswell, P.R.; *British Trolleybuses*; Ian Allan Ltd; 1967
Trolleybus Magazine; National Trolleybus Association
Turner, Keith, Smith, Paul and Smith, Shirley; *The Directory of British Tram Depots*; OPC; 2001
Wells; Malcolm; *Kingston upon Hull Trolleybuses*; Trolleybooks; 1996